natural knits
for babies & toddlers

natural knits
for babies & toddlers

tina barrett

GUILD OF MASTER
CRAFTSMAN PUBLICATIONS

First published 2008 by

Guild of Master Craftsman Publications Ltd.
Castle Place, 166 High Street,
Lewes, East Sussex BN7 1XU

Reprinted 2010

Text and designs © Tina Barrett, 2008

© in the Work GMC Publications Ltd, 2008

ISBN 978-1-86108-559-7

Associate Publisher **Jonathan Bailey**
Production Manager **Jim Bulley**
Managing Editor **Gerrie Purcell**
Project Editor **Virginia Brehaut**
Managing Art Editor **Gilda Pacitti**
Photographer **Chris Gloag**

Set in Avant Garde and American Typewriter

Colour origination by GMC Reprographics
Printed and bound in Thailand by KNP

contents

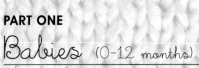

PART THREE

Accessories

PART FOUR

Knitting basics

introduction

This book was inspired by the birth of my fourth child, Lily. There are sixteen years between her and my eldest daughter. You don't need to be a mathematician to figure out that's a rather large age gap. Needless to say, when I found out I was expecting again, it was a bit of a surprise! It didn't take any of us long to get over it and we soon embraced the idea of a new arrival to the family. I was older, wiser and this time, determined to enjoy her early years rather than stressing about teething, potty training, weaning and all that other self-induced angst that new motherhood brings.

As the whole family prepared for her entry into the world, we realized we were no longer equipped for a baby. Prams and cots were passed on long ago. We had no sterilizers, soothers or toys. We would have to start from scratch. It had been eight long years since I'd set foot in a baby shop. And in eight years, things had changed – a lot!

When it came to bottoms, disposable nappies were now *out* and washable nappies *in*. As for weaning, jars were out and home cooked, organic food in. And clothing… well, soft, natural and organic fibres were the only thing mums wanted to put their precious bundles in. But then more to the point, so did I!

Amidst the increased awareness of global warming and climate change, I suddenly realized it was time to make far more pro-active choices for all my children, including little Lily; choices which might even positively affect – albeit in some small way – their future environment.

So, I set out on a journey. I knew I wanted to create beautiful things for my baby but within those designs I was determined to use only natural fibres processed in the most gentle, organic way which would leave only a baby-sized eco footprint on the world after they had been produced. As well as beautifully soft yarn that would be kind to my baby's skin, I also wanted colour because bright, rainbow colours are a fundamental part of a child's world.

Well, it's been an exciting and complex journey and this book of designs is the result. I have gained much pleasure (and indeed insight) during the process and met some wonderful people along the way who share the whole same vision and integrity about their yarns and notions.

I really hope these pages inspire you and that you find something gorgeous within them to knit for your own little miracle. Everyone who has contributed to this book has taken care of the bigger picture, all you need take care of now are the stitches.

Happy knitting,

Tina Barrett

natural yarns & fibres

Why go natural? Okay, it's a fair question. After all, those acrylic and polyester fibres have come a long way since their squeaky, static-prone origins. Man-made yarns will always have their place in the market but there is undoubtedly a growing number of knitters who are sourcing natural fibres for their projects.

Wool

The most familiar fibre to all knitters. Organic wool is produced without the use of organo-phosphate dips and the sheep must be free to roam and have rotational grazing. After these happy sheep have been shorn, the wool is hand-sorted and 'finished' without acids, shrink-proofing, bleaches or moth-proofing. Only vegetable-based soaps are used within the washing process so the finished skein is as pure and natural as possible.

Bamboo

We are seeing major yarn manufacturers embracing bamboo fibre. The yarn is wonderfully soft and breathable. I have used it in the nursing pads because of this very fact. However, it also has naturally occurring anti-bacterial properties and is UV protective. Knitting to a DK weight, it produces a lovely soft, draping fabric.

Hemp

Grown naturally and without pesticides or herbicides, hemp has the added benefit of being a nitrogen fixer which means that it improves the soil as it grows. The yarn is string-like in texture but grows softer and lovelier the more you handle it. The drape of the fabric it produces is wonderful, although it is not terribly elastic. The vivid colours in this book are obtained using earth-friendly dyes and a natural, not metal-based mordant.

A fantastic reason for using natural yarns is your baby's skin. A baby's skin is soft, sensitive and gorgeous. Therefore, it makes perfect sense to choose soft, natural, breathable fibres to put next to it. By that, I mean fibres that won't irritate and haven't been treated with harsh dyes or processed with chemicals. Natural fibres are often perfect for those with allergies and sensitive skin.

Another reason for choosing natural yarns is that they come from sustainable sources, they avoid the use of artificial fertilizers, herbicides, fungicides or organo-phosphate dips and they can be produced with minimal pollution and therefore have a very low impact on the surrounding environment. So that's excellent news for the health of the planet and for the babies and toddlers we're knitting for too!

Alpaca

Alpaca is growing in popularity with knitters and yarn manufacturers. The alpaca is a commonly found in Peru and is said to be the warmest fibre on earth – indeed, it is indescribably soft and fluffy. A lightweight DK ply, it gives a luxurious finish which is great for a wide variety of projects. Alpaca is lanolin and dander free giving it naturally hypo-allergenic properties. All this makes it perfect for babies and anyone sensitive to pure wool.

Cotton

The cotton industry has had bad press over its use of artificial pesticides and fertilizers and heavy chemical processing. However, cotton is a popular choice for the knitter. It shows texture well and gives a classic finish. I have chosen a good quality, organic cotton yarn. The colours are undyed and come in naturally occurring plant shades. It is soft and chunky to work with and a good substitute for the more commercially grown alternatives.

Corn fibre

I had never used corn fibre before starting this book and was dying to have a fiddle around with it. I was delighted to find it resembled ribbon yarn and had an almost cotton-like finish when knitted up. Dyed with earth-friendly colours and in DK weight, this fibre had the added bonus of being able to be chucked in the washer and then the dryer which is always good news when you've got toddlers learning to feed themselves!

Babies

(0-12 months)

wool baby nest
pattern page 56

cotton pram
blanket
pattern page 52

cotton toy dog

pattern page 53

alpaca cardigan,
hat & bootees
pattern page 64

corn fibre sleep sack

pattern page 58

cotton cardigan,
beanie & mittens
pattern page 60

cotton cardigan,
beanie & mittens
pattern page 60

corn fibre
striped rompers
pattern page 68

corn fibre
striped rompers
pattern page 68

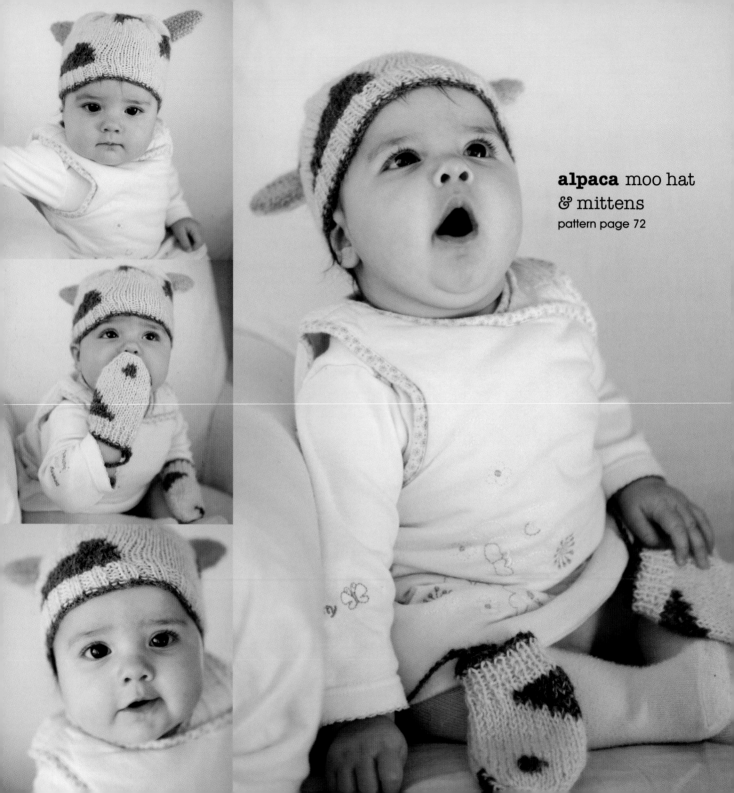

alpaca moo hat
& mittens
pattern page 72

alpaca comfort
blankies
pattern page 76

Toddlers
(1-3 years)

corn fibre
lace pyjamas
pattern page 80

corn fibre
hooded gilet
pattern page 84

hemp swing
dress & trousers
pattern page 102

corn fibre
hooded gilet
pattern page 84

wool cable
jumper &
earflap hat
pattern page 88

wool cable jumper
& earflap hat
pattern page 88

hemp t-shirt & combat pants

pattern page 90

hemp t-shirt & combat pants
pattern page 90

alpaca
cardigan & beret
pattern page 94

hemp swing dress & trousers
pattern page 102

wool aran cable jumper

pattern page 98

wool earflap hats
patterns pages 88 and 108

wool tank top & hat
pattern page 106

Accessories

changing bag
& bottle tote
pattern page 112

changing bag
pattern page 112

corn fibre
burp cloth & bib
pattern page 116

soy silk nappy liner

pattern page 120

bamboo nursing pads
pattern page 122

alpaca lavender pillow
pattern page 124

PART ONE

Babies

(0–12 months)

cotton pram blanket & toy dog

Here's a snugly cotton blanket for keeping warm whilst out and about in the pram. A cute matching toy dog is filled with organic stuffing and fully washable so you can keep him nice and clean when he's had a little too much loving.

Sizes

Blanket 32 x 25½in (81 x 65cm)
Toy dog 9in (23cm)

Materials

BLANKET
Blue Sky Alpacas Organic Cotton
100% organic cotton (137m/150yd per 100g ball)
2 x 100g balls in Sage
4 x 100g balls in Bone
5.5mm (US9) 31½in (80cm) circular needle
2in (5cm) diameter card circles or pompom makers

TOY DOG
Blue Sky Alpacas Organic Cotton
1 x 100g ball in Bone
1 x 100g ball in Sage
5mm (US8) needles
Cornish Organic Wool, Organic Toy Stuffing
Small amount of black thread for embroidery.
Stitch holder

Tension

16 sts over 4in (10cm) for blanket

Blanket

Using 5.5mm circular needle and Bone, cast on 142 sts. Use circular needle as if straight pair, working back and forth across each row.

Row 1 K2, purl to last 2 sts, k2.
Row 2 K1, kfb, k4, sl1, k1, psso, k2tog, k4 *(kfb, kfb, k4, sl1, k1, psso, k2tog, k4) rep from * to last 2 sts, kfb, k1.
These 2 rows form the zig-zag pattern.
Rep, working the stripe sequence as follows:
3in (8cm) in Bone
2in (5cm) in Sage
Rep this stripe sequence 5 times.
Finally, work 3in (8cm) in Bone.
Cast off.

MAKING UP
Darn in all loose yarn ends. Press lightly. Make 18 x 2in (5cm) pompoms *(see page 137 for instructions)* as follows:

9 in Bone and 9 in Sage.
Fasten the pompoms to each point, alternating the colours.

Toy dog

HEAD (make 1)

Using 5mm (US8) needles and Bone, cast on 4 sts.

Row 1 Kfb into every st (8 sts).
Row 2 and every alt row Purl.
Row 3 Kfb into every st (16 sts).
Row 5 *(K1, kfb,) rep from * to end of row (24 sts).
Row 7 As row 5 (36 sts).
Beg with a knit row, st st for 6 rows.

Dec as follows:
Row 1 (K4, k2tog) rep from * to end of row (30 sts).
Row 2 and every alt row Purl.
Row 3 *(K3, k2tog) rep from * to end of row (24 sts).
Row 5 *(K2, k2tog) rep from * to end of row (18 sts).
Row 7 *(K1, k2tog) rep from * to end of row (12 sts).
Row 9 K2tog to end of row (6 sts).
Row 10 K2tog to end of row (3 sts).
Break yarn, leaving a long tail, thread through rem 3 sts and pull tight.
Sew rear seam leaving a small hole for stuffing.
Stuff fairly firmly with organic stuffing and sew up the hole.

EARS (make 2 alike)

Using 5mm (US8) needles and Sage, cast on 3 sts.

Row 1 Kfb, p1, kfb (5 sts).
Row 2 *(p1, k1) rep from * to end.
Rep row 2, 3 more times.
Row 6 Krb, k1, p1, k1, kfb (7 sts).
Row 7 *(K1, p1) rep from * to end.
Rep row 7 until ear measures 2in (5cm).
Next row P2tog, patt to last 2 sts, p2tog (5 sts).
Next row (P1, k1) rep from * to end.
Next row P2 tog, patt to last 2 sts, p2tog (3 sts).
Next row K1, p1, k1.
Next row P3 tog.
Break yarn, thread through rem st and fasten off.

BODY

First Leg

Using 5mm (US8) needles and Bone, cast on 8 sts.

Row 1 Kfb into each st (16 sts).
Beg with a purl row, st st for 2in (5cm) ending on a purl row.
Break yarn and leave st on a spare needle.

Second Leg

Work the second leg in the same way as the first.

Body

With RS of work facing, knit across the 16 sts of first leg then across the 16 sts of the second leg (32 sts).

Beg with a purl row, work straight in st st for a further 2in (5cm).

Shape shoulders
Row 1 (K6, k2tog) rep from * to end (28 sts).
Row 2 and every alt row Purl.
Row 3 (K5, k2tog) rep from * to end (24 sts).
Row 5 (K4, k2tog) rep from * to end (20 sts).
Row 7 (K3, k2tog) rep from * to end (16 sts).
Row 9 (K2, k2tog) rep from * to end (12 sts).
Row 10 K2 tog to end (6 sts).
Break yarn, leaving a long tail, thread through rem sts and pull tight.
Turn the body RS in and sew rear seam, leaving a small hole for stuffing.
Turn RS out and stuff fairly firmly with organic stuffing. Sew up the opening.

ARMS (make 2 alike)

Using 5mm (US8) needles and Bone, cast on 8 sts leaving a long tail.

Row 1 Kfb into each st (16 sts).

Beg with a purl row, work in st st for 2in (5cm), ending on a purl row.

Cast off.

Turn RS in. Gather cast on edges of arm and pull tight and fasten off. Sew rear seam. Turn RS out and stuff the arm fairly firmly.

NOSE

Using 5mm (US8) needles and Sage, cast on 2 sts.

Row 1 Kfb into each st (4 sts).

Row 2 Purl.

Row 3 (K1, kfb) twice (6 sts).

Row 4 Purl.

Row 5 (K1, k2tog) twice (4 sts).

Row 6 Purl.

Row 7 K2 tog twice (2 sts).

Break yarn, leaving a tail, thread through rem sts and pull tight.

With a few neat stitches, sew up rear seam and gather the cast off edge and cast on edges together so the nose forms a compact bobble.

Fasten off.

SWEATER

Front and back (work 2 pieces alike)

Using 5mm (US8) needles and Sage, cast on 23 sts.

Working in st st and beg with a knit row, work stripe patt as folls:

2 rows Sage

2 rows Bone

Rep this stripe patt 5 times (20 rows in total).

Shape shoulders

Cast off 4 sts, place centre 15 sts on holder, cast off 4 sts.

Sleeves (make 2 alike)

Cast on 22 sts in Sage.

Work stripe patt twice (8 rows in total).

Cast off.

Neckband

Sew right shoulder seam.

With RS facing and Sage, knit across neck sts from front and back holders (30 sts).

Work 3 rows in st st.

Cast off.

Darn in loose yarn ends and sew neck, arm and side seams to finish.

MAKING UP

Place the head on the shoulders. Sew firmly in place with small neat stitches around the neck. Pin both arms in place at shoulder height, and sew firmly in place. Place the ears near the top of the head *(see photo)* and sew neatly in place. Sew nose to centre of face. Embroider both eyes with black embroidery thread using a single Swiss darning stitch *(see page 138 for instructions)*. Using back stitch *(see page 138)*, embroider the mouth. Refer to the photo for guidance. Finally, dress the dog in his new sweater.

knitknack

As with all toys designed for young children, make sure seams are sewn securely so stuffing cannot escape. Check seams from time to time and darn them if necessary.

safe stuffing

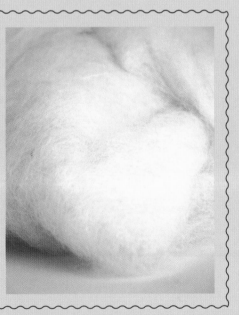

Using organic stuffing means that your projects will be chemical-free through and through. It is washed and combed without the use of any harsh chemicals and can also be used for spinning and felting.

wool baby nest

Snuggle baby up in this toasty organic wool cocoon with pretty heart-shaped buttons. It is perfect for those outdoor adventures when it is chilly and baby needs to be kept warm and secure.

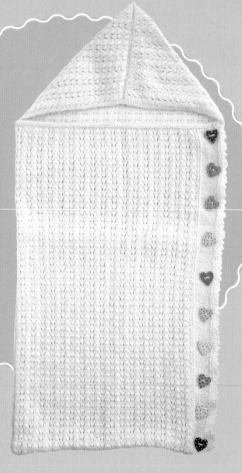

Sizes

	0–3 months		3–6 months	
Finished width	10in	25cm	12in	30.5cm
Length from top of hood	26in	66cm	28in	71cm

Materials

3 x 100g skeins of Cornish Organic 4-ply wool in Natural (336m/367yd per 100g skein)
10 heart buttons (by Stockwell Pottery, see *Suppliers* page 142)
3mm (US3) needles
3mm (US3) 31½in (80cm) circular needles

Tension

26 sts x 40 rows to 4in (10cm) over Little Fountain pattern

Baby nest

BACK

Cast on 65[77] sts.

Beg Little Fountain Patt as follows:

Row 1(RS) K1 *yf, k3,yf, k1, rep from * to end.

Row 2 Purl.

Row 3 K2, sl1, k2tog, psso *k3, sl1, k2tog, psso; rep from * to last 2 sts, k2.

Row 4 Purl.

Rep these 4 rows until work measures 26[28]in (66[71]cm), ending on a WS row.

Cast off.

FRONT

Cast on 57[73] sts.

Work Little Fountain patt as for back until work measures 19[21]in (48[53.5]cm) ending on a WS row.

Cast off.

Front Buttonhole Border

Using 3mm (US3) needles, with RS facing PUK 124[156] sts along right side edge of front.

Garter st 3 rows.

Beg with a knit row, st st for 6 rows.

Buttonhole row K2[4], cast off 3 sts, *k10[11], cast off 3 sts; rep from * to last 2[3] sts, k2[3].

Next row Purl, casting on 3 sts at every buttonhole (ie. where you cast off 3 sts on the previous row).

Beg with a knit row, st st 3 rows.

Garter st 3 rows.

Picot cast off as follows:

Cast off 2 sts, *return sts to left-hand needle. Cast on 2 sts using the cable cast on method *(see page 130 for details)*, cast off 4 sts, rep from * to end of row.

MAKING UP

Pin and block both pieces. Darn in any loose yarn ends. Fold the top edges of back piece to centre and sew short seam to form hood. Pin and sew front and back pieces along bottom and left side edge. Mark position of buttons and sew securely in position on WS of back piece down the right edge.

Hood edging

Using 3mm (US3) circular needles and with RS facing, PUK 78 sts along top front edge and 78 sts from around hood (156 sts).

Garter st 2 rows.

Cast off.

Darn in loose yarn ends.

knitknack

If it is extra cold outside, you could line this baby nest with organic jersey or another fabric for added snugness.

corn fibre sleep sack

This project is both pretty and practical. It is designed to fit baby from birth right up until six months and with no fiddly legs or poppers, the decorative ties make nappy changing quick and easy.

Size

	0–6 months	
Finished chest	20in	51cm
Finished length from shoulder	28in	71cm
Sleeve length (to armhole)	6½in	16.5cm

Materials

SWTC Amazing 100% Corn fibre
(130m/142yd per 50g ball)
6 x 50g balls in Cream Puff
1 x 50g ball in Keepsake
4 x heart buttons (by Injabulo,
see *Suppliers* page 142)
3.75mm (US5) needles
4.5mm (US7) needles

Tension

24 sts x 32 rows over 4in (10cm)

Sleep sack

FRONT AND BACK

(make 2 pieces alike)

Using 3.75mm (US5) needles and Keepsake, cast on 61 sts.

Change to Cream Puff and k1 row.

Eyelet Row K5, yf, k2tog *(k8, yf, k2tog) rep from * 3 times, k8, yf, k2tog, k4.

Change to 4mm (US7) needles and beg Diamond patt as follows:

Row 1 K3 *(p1, k5) rep from * to last 4sts, p1, k3.

Row 2 P2 *(k1, p1, k1, p3) rep from * to last 5 sts, k1, p1, k1, p2.

Row 3 K1 *(p1, k3, p1, k1) rep from * to end.

Row 4 k1 *(p5, k1) rep from * to end.

Row 5 k1 *(p1, k3, p1, k1) rep from * to end.

Row 6 p2 *(k1, p1, k1, p3) rep from * to last 5 sts, k1, p1, k1, p2.

Rep diamond patt until work meas 23in (58.5cm), ending on a WS row.

Shape Raglan

Keeping to patt, cast off 3 sts at beg of next 2 rows (55 sts).

Dec 1 st at each end of next and alt rows until 19 sts, ending on a WS row.

Garter st 4 rows.

Cast off in Keepsake.

SLEEVES (make 2 alike)

Using 3.75mm (US5) needles and Keepsake, cast on 37 sts.

Change to Cream Puff and garter st 2 rows.

Change to 4.5mm (US7) needles and beg diamond patt as for front, at the same time inc 1 st at each end of next and every foll 4th row until 59 sts.

Work straight until sleeve measures 6½in (16.5cm), ending on a WS row.

Shape Raglan

Keeping to patt, cast off 3 sts at beg of next 2 rows (53 sts).

Dec 1 st at each end of next and every foll alt row until 15 sts rem, ending on a WS row.

Garter st 4 rows.

Cast off in Keepsake.

MAKING UP

Darn in any loose yarn ends.

Pin and sew one side of sleeve raglans to back piece of sleep sack.

Sleeve bands

Using 3.75mm (US5) needles and Cream Puff and with RS facing, PUK 28 sts along front edge of sleeve raglan.

Garter st 5 rows.

Cast off. Darn in loose ends.

Rep for other sleeve.

Front buttonhole bands

Using 3.75mm (US5) needles and Cream Puff and with RS facing, PUK 28 sts along right front raglan.

Garter st 1 row

Buttonhole row K4, cast off 2 sts, k8, cast off 2 sts, k10.

Next row K10, cast on 2 sts, k8, cast on 2 sts, k4.

K2 rows.

Cast off.

Rep for left front raglan with buttonhole row as follows:

Buttonhole row K10 sts, cast off 2 sts, k8, cast off 2 sts, k4.

Next row K10, cast on 2 sts, k8, cast on 2 sts, k4.

Mark position of buttons on sleeve bands and sew firmly in place. Button to front bands.

Pin and sew sleeve and side seams of baby sleep sack.

Tie

Using 6 strands of Keepsake, make a plaited tie 30in (76cm) long. Thread through eyelets at bottom of sack and pull tight.

cotton cardigan, beanie & mittens

This stripy, ribbed and moss-stitched set has a matching hat and button-on mittens for the chilliest of weather. Knitted in softest organic cotton, it is both warm and snugly to the touch and includes sizing for premature babies too.

Sizes

	early (up to 5lb)	0–3 months	3–6 months	6–12 months
Finished chest	16in	18in	20in	22in
	41cm	46cm	51cm	56cm
Sleeve length	5in	6in	6½in	8in
	13cm	15cm	16.5cm	20.5cm
Length from shoulder	8in	9½in	10½in	11½in
	20.5cm	24cm	27cm	29cm
Head circumference	11in	12in	14in	18in
	28cm	30.5cm	35.5cm	46cm

Materials

Blue Sky Alpacas Organic Cotton DK
(231m/252yd per 100g ball)
2[3:3:4] balls in Bone
2[2:2:3] balls in Sage
4.5 mm (US7) needles
Stitch holder
5[7:8:8] wood buttons

Tension

20 sts x 24 rows to 4in (10cm)

Cardigan

BACK

Using Sage and 4.5mm (US7) needles cast on 40[44:52:56] sts.
Change to Bone.
Row 1 P1(k2, p2) rep bracket seq to last st, p1.
Row 2 K1*(p2, k2) rep from * to last st, k1.
These 2 rows form the double rib patt.
Work in patt until work measures 3½ [4½ :5½ :5]in (9[11.5:14:13]cm), ending

on a row 2.

Change to Sage.

Work straight until back measures 4½ [5½ :6½ :7½]in (11.5[14:16.5:19]cm), ending on a row 2.

Shape armholes

Cast off 3[4:3:3] sts at beg of next 2 rows 34[36:46:50] sts.

Work a further 1[1:1:1½]in (2.5[2.5:2.5:4]cm) in Sage ending on a row 2.

Change to Bone.

Work straight until back measures 8[9½:10½:11½]in (20.5[24:27:29]cm), ending on WS row.

Shape shoulders

Patt 10[10:14:15], turn.

Work on these sts only.

Row 1 K2tog, patt to end 9[9:13:14] sts.

Cast off.

Slip centre 14[16:18:20] sts onto a stitch holder.

Rejoin to second side.

Row 1 Patt to end.

Row 2 Patt to last 2 sts, k2tog, 9[9:13:14] sts.

Cast off.

LEFT FRONT

Using 4.5mm (US7) needles and Sage cast on 16[18:22:24] sts.

Change to Bone.

Work as for back, including the stripe detail up to armhole.

Shape armhole

Cast off 3 sts at beg of next row 13[15:19:21] sts.

Keeping to patt and incorporating the stripe, work until front is 9[11:13:13] rows less than back, ending on a WS row.

Shape neck

Next row Dec 1 st on next and foll alt rows until 9[9:13:14] sts rem.

Work even until front armhole matches back.

Cast off.

RIGHT FRONT

Work as for left front, reversing all shapings.

SLEEVES

Using Sage and 4.5mm (US7) needles, cast on 24[28:28:32] sts.

Change to Bone.

Work rib patt as set inc 1 st at each end of foll 3rd and then 4th row until 34[36:40:48] sts.

At same time work stripe by changing to Sage when sleeve measures 2[3:3½:3]in (5[8:9:8]cm). Work a 2[2:2:3]in (5[5:5:8]cm) stripe before changing back to Bone.

After increases are complete, work straight until sleeve measures 5[6:6½:8]in (13[15:16.5:20.5]cm), ending on a row 2.

Cast off.

COLLAR

Sew shoulder seams.

With RS facing and using Bone, PUK 8[10:12:13] sts along right front edge, 3 sts down back neck, 14[16:18:20] sts from back stitch holder, 3 sts up back of left neck and 8[10:12:13] sts down left front edge (36[42:48:52] sts). Work double rib patt as set for 1½[2:2:2½]in (4[5:5:6.5]cm), ending on a row 2.

Cast off loosely in Sage.

RIGHT FRONT BAND

Cast off 5 sts in Sage.

Change to Bone.

Work in moss st until front band fits right front edge of cardigan.

Cast off.

Darn in loose yarn ends and sew to front.

Mark button positions.

LEFT FRONT BAND

Make 2nd band to match, working buttonholes to correspond with button positions on right band as follows:

Buttonhole rows Moss st 2, yo, k2tog, moss st 1.

Sew in place.

MAKING UP

Darn in loose yarn ends.

Pin and sew sleeves in place.

Sew side seams.

Sew buttons onto right front band.

Sew a button on the upper part of each sleeve cuff for mitts.

Beanie

Using 4.5mm (US7) needles and Sage, cast off 52[56:60:84] sts
Change to Bone
Work in moss st for 1in (2.5cm).
Change to Sage.
Moss stitch 1½[1½:1½:2]in (4[4:4:5]cm).
Change to Bone.
Work even until hat measures 3[3½:4:5]in (8[9:10:13]cm).

Dec for crown

Row 1 *(k2, k2tog) rep from * to end 39[42:45:63] sts.
Row 2 and all alt rows Moss st.
Row 3 *(k1, k2tog) rep from * to end 26[28:30:42] sts.
Row 5 *k2tog rep from * to end 13[14:15:21] sts.
Row 7 K1[0:1:1], *k2tog rep from * to end 7[7:8:11] sts.
Row 9 K1[1:0:1], *k2tog rep from * to end 4[4:4:6] sts.
Break yarn, thread through rem sts and pull tight.
Sew up rear seam.

Mittens

(make 2)
Using 4.5mm (US7) needles and Sage, cast on 20[26:30:32] sts.
Change to Bone.

Buttonhole row

1st size K2, p2, yf, k2tog, *(p2,k2) rep from * to end.
2nd/3rd size K2, p2, k2, yf, p2tog, *(k2, p2) rep from * to end.
4th size K2, p2, k2, p2, yf, k2tog, (p2, k2) rep from * to end.
Work in double rib for 1[1:1:1½]in (2.5[2.5:2.5:4]cm).
Change to moss stitch.
Work straight in moss stitch until mitt measures 2¾[3:3½:3½]in (7[8:9:9]cm).

Shape top

Next row *Sl 1, k1, psso, moss st 6[9:11:12] k2tog rep from * twice 16[22:26:28] sts.
Next and alt rows Moss st.
Next row *Sl 1, k1, psso, moss st 4[7:9:10] k2tog, rep from * twice 12[18:22:24] sts.
1st size only Cast off.
2nd/3rd/4th sizes *Sl1, k1, psso, moss st 5[7:8], k2tog, rep from * twice 14[18:20] sts.
Cast off.
Sew side seam.

knitknack

Remember, size matters when it comes to selecting buttons. Try to find small buttons when knitting tiny or newborn sizes. Keep larger buttons for larger sizes so everything remains in proportion. Make sure they are always sewn on securely.

alpaca cardigan, hat & bootees

This pretty set is knitted in warm, soft alpaca – a perfect gift for new babies.
Slip on the cardigan over a cute dress with the hat and bootees for a glamorous
journey out in the pram. Includes a premature size for early arrivals.

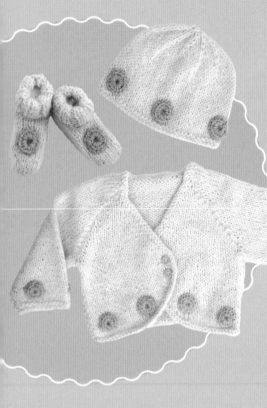

Sizes

	early (up to 5lb)	0–6 months	6–12 months
Finished chest	16in	20in	22in
	41cm	51cm	56cm
Length from shoulder	7in	9in	10in
	18cm	23cm	25.5cm
Sleeve length	4¾in	7in	8in
	12cm	18cm	20.5cm
Hat circumference	11in	14in	16in
	28cm	36cm	41cm

Materials

Artesano Inca Mist (120m /131yd per
50g ball)
3[4:5] x 50g balls in Cream
1[1:1] x 50g ball in Baby Pink
3.25 (US4) needles
4mm (US6) needles
3.25mm (US4) circular needle
3.5mm (USE/4) crochet hook
2 x small pink buttons (by Stockwell
Pottery, see *Suppliers*, page 142)

Tension

25 sts x 33 rows over 4in (10cm)

Cardigan

BACK

Using 4mm (US6) needles and Cream, cast on 50[62:68] sts.

Work even in st st until work measures 3½[5:5½]in (9[13:14]cm), ending on a WS row.

Shape raglan

Cast off 3 sts at beg of next 2 rows. 44[56:62] sts.

Dec 1 st at each end of next and foll alt rows until 18[24:26] sts, ending on a WS row.

Cast off.

LEFT FRONT

Using 4mm (US6) needles, cast on 17[20:22] sts.

St st 2 rows.

Row 1 Knit to end: cast on 2 sts, 19[22:24] sts.

Row 2 Purl.

Rep last 2 rows 5[5:6] times. 27[30:34] sts.

Next row Knit to last st, inc 1, 28[31:35] sts.

Next row Purl.

Rep last 2 rows 2[5:4] more times. 30[36:39] sts.

*Work even in st st for 8[10:12] rows.**

1st and 3rd sizes only

Next row Knit.

Next row Cast off 2 sts, purl to end 28[37] sts.

Rep these 2 rows once more 26[35] sts

2nd and 3rd sizes only

Next row Knit to last 2 sts, k2tog.

Next Purl.

Rep these last 2 rows 5[3]times. 31[32] sts.

Shape armholes (all sizes)

Row 1 Cast off 3 sts at beg of row, knit to last 0[2:2] sts: k0[2:2]tog. 23[27:28] sts.

Next row Purl.

Shape neck

Dec 1 st at each end of next and foll alt rows 3[3:1] times, ending on a purl row. 17[21:26] sts.

Next row Dec 1st at armhole edge on next and foll alt rows, at same time dec 1 st at neck edge on next and foll 4th rows until 3[3:2] sts, ending on a purl row.

1st and 2nd sizes only

Next row K1, k2tog [2 sts].

Next row P2tog.

Fasten off.

3rd size

St st 2 rows.

K2tog.

Fasten off.

RIGHT FRONT

Work as for left front reversing shapings until *.

Work 2 rows st st.

Buttonhole row K2, yf, k2tog, knit to end

Next row Purl.

St st 2[2:4] rows.

Rep buttonhole row.

Work 1[3:3] rows st st.

Continue working as for left front from ** to end, reversing all shapings.

SLEEVES

Using 3.25mm (US4) needles and Cream, cast on 32[36:40] sts.
Garter stitch 2 rows. Change to 4mm (US6) needles.
Inc 1 st at each end of next and every foll 6th row until 44[50:56] sts.
Work even until sleeve measures 4¾[7:8]in (12[18:20.5]cm), ending on a WS row.

Shape raglan

Cast off 3 sts at beg of next 2 rows. 38[44:50] sts.
Dec 1 st at each end of next 2 rows 34[40:46] sts.
Dec 1 st at each end of foll alt rows until 8[10:12] sts ending, on a WS row.
Cast off.

MAKING UP

Pin and block pieces. Darn in loose yarn ends. Sew raglans, side and sleeve seams.

Neckband

With RS facing, using 3.25mm (US4) circular needle and Cream, PUK 50[62:68] sts along lower edge of back, 55[75:85] sts up curved edge of right front to sleeve head, 4[5:6] sts across sleeve, 12[16:18] sts across back of neck, 4[5:6] sts across second sleeve and 55[75:85] sts down curved edge of left front. 180[238:268] sts.
Garter st 3 rows.
Cast off loosely.
Sew on buttons.
Position crochet motifs around lower edge of cardigan and sleeves (see numbers required below). Slip stitch neatly in place.

Crochet Motifs

Using 3.5mm (USE/4) crochet hook and Baby Pink make a ch of 5.
Join the ring with a slip stitch.
Round 1 1ch, 15htr into centre. Slip stitch into first chain to join round.
Fasten off.

Motif numbers

Cardigan 3[4:4] per sleeve.
2[3:3] per front.
4[5:6] per back.
14[19:20] in total.
Bootees 2 in total.
Hat 6[7:8] in total.

Hat

Using 3.25mm (US4) needles and
Cream, cast on 66[84:96] sts.
Garter stitch 2 rows.
Change to 4mm (US6) needles.
Work even in st st until hat measures
3½[4½:5½]in (9[11.5:14]cm) ending
on a WS row.

Decrease for crown

Row 1 (K4,k2tog) rep to end.
55[70:80] sts.

Row 2 and alt rows Purl

Row 3 (K3,k2tog) rep to end.
44[56:64] sts.

Row 5 (K2, k2tog) rep to end.
33[42:48] sts.

Row 7 (K1,k2tog) rep to end.
22[28:32] sts.

Row 9 K2tog to end. 11[14:16] sts.

Row 11 K1[0:0], k2tog to end. 6[7:8] sts
Break yarn, leaving a long tail, thread
yarn through rem st and pull tight.
Pin and block hat, darn in loose yarn
ends and sew rear seam.
Position crochet motifs and slip stitch
neatly in place.

Bootees

CUFF

Using 3.25mm (US4) needles and Baby
Pink, cast on 24[37:43] sts.
Change to Cream.
Work k1, p1 rib for 2[2½:3]in
(5[6.5:8]cm).

Divide for upper

K17[25:30] sts.
P10[15:17] sts working on these sts only,
st st for 2[2½:2¾]in (5[6:7.5]cm) ending
on a purl row. Break yarn.
With RS facing 7[12:13] sts on needle,
rejoin yarn and PUK 11[15:18] sts along
side of foot, 10[15:17] sts from toe,
11[15:18] sts along side of foot and
7[12:13] sts on needle. 46[69:79] sts.

Next row Purl.
Work 6[10:12] rows in stocking stitch.

Shape sole

1st size only

Row 1 K2, k2tog, k16,k2tog, k1,k2tog,
knit to end.

Row 2 K2, k2tog, knit to end.

Row 3 K2, k2tog, k14, k2tog, k1, k2tog,
knit to end.

Row 4 As row 2.

Row 5 K2, k2tog, k12, k2tog, k1, k2tog,
knit to end.

Row 6 As row 2.
Cast off.

2nd and 3rd sizes only

Row 1 K1*k2tog, k28[33], k2tog*k3,
work * to * again, k1. 65[75] sts.

Row 2 K29[34], k2tog, k3, k2tog,
k29[34]. 63[73] sts.

Row 3 K1*k2tog, k25[30], k2tog*k3,
work *to* again, k1. 59[69] sts.

Row 4 K26[31], k2tog, k3,
k2tog,k26[31]. 57[67] sts.

Row 5 K1*k2tog, k22[27], k2tog*k3,
work * to * again, k1. 53[63] sts.
Cast off.

MAKING UP

Press bootees lightly. Darn in loose
yarn ends.
Sew sole and rear seam. Fold down
cuff and position crochet motif on
front of shoe.
Slip stitch neatly in place.

corn fibre striped rompers

These classic, striped rompers come in a short-sleeved version for summer babies and a long-sleeved version with fold-over mitts for winter babies. Plus, there are enough sizes to keep you knitting right through their early months.

Sizes

	early (up to 5lb)	0–3 months	3–6 months	6–12 months
Finished chest	16in	18in	20in	22in
	41cm	46cm	51cm	56cm
Length from shoulder (short)	12in	17in	18in	20½in
	30.5cm	43cm	46cm	52cm
Length from shoulder (long)	14½in	20in	22in	24½in
	37cm	51cm	56cm	62cm
Sleeve length (short)	2in	2½in	2½in	3in
	5cm	6.5cm	6.5cm	8cm
Sleeve length (long)	5in	6½in	7½in	8½in
	13cm	16.5cm	19cm	22cm
Leg length (short)	2½in	3in	4in	5in
	6.5cm	8cm	10cm	13cm
Leg length (long)	5in	7in	8in	9in
	13cm	18cm	20.5cm	23cm

Materials

SWTC Amaizing 100% Corn fibre, (130m/142yd per 50g ball)

SHORT-SLEEVED VERSION
Cream Puff (MC) 2[3:3:4] x 50g balls
Grenadine (CC) 1[1:2:2] x 50g balls
5[7:8:10] wood buttons

LONG-SLEEVED VERSION
Cream Puff (MC) 2[3:4:5] x 50g balls
Atlantis (CC) 2[3:4:4] x 50 g balls

9[11:14:14] wood buttons
3.75mm (US5) and 4.5mm (US7) needles
2 stitch holders

Tension

24 sts x 32 rows to 4in (10cm)

Rompers

BACK

Right leg

Using CC and 3.75mm needles, cast on 18[20:24:28] sts.

Work moss st patt for 4 rows.

Change to 4.5mm (US7) needles and MC and beg with a knit row, start stripe sequence in st st as follows:

6 rows MC, 2 rows CC

at same time inc 1st on right edge on next and every 4th row until 24[26:30:34] sts.

Work straight in stripe patt until leg measures 2½[3:4:5]in (6.5[8:10:13]cm) for short-legged version and 5[7:8:9] in 13[18:20.5:23]cm for long-legged version, ending on a WS row.

Break yarn and leave sts on spare needle.

Left leg

Work as for right leg but make the increases at left edge of work.

Body

With RS of work facing, slide right leg and then left leg onto a 4.5mm (US7) needle.

Keeping to stripe patt, work straight across both legs 48[52:60:68] sts.

Cont working even in stripe patt until body (from crotch upwards) measures 6[9:10:11]in (15[23:25:28]cm), ending on a WS row.

Shape armholes

Cast off 3 sts at beg of next 2 rows. 42[46:54:62]sts.

Work even in st st until armhole measures 3½[4:4:4½]in (9[10:10:11.5] cm), ending on a WS row.

Shape shoulders

K12[13:15:18]. Turn.

Working on these sts only, p2tog, purl to end of row. 11[12:14:17] sts.

Cast off.

Slip centre 18[20:24:26] sts onto holder. Rejoin yarn to second side. Knit to end.

Next row P10[11:13:16], p2tog 11[12:14:17] sts.

Button band

Change to 3.75mm (US5) needles and CC.

Moss st 4 rows.

Cast off.

FRONT

Work as for back until 10[12:14:14] rows less than back.

Patt 15[16:18:21] sts. Turn.

Dec 1 st at neck edge on next and every foll row until 11[12:14:17] sts.

Work even until armhole measure 2 rows less than back.

Buttonhole band

Change to 3.75mm needles and CC.

Rows 1 & 2 Moss st.

Row 3 1st and 2nd sizes only: Patt 4[5] yo, k2tog, patt 5[5].

3rd and 4th sizes only Patt 4[5] yo, k2tog, patt 3[4], yo, k2tog, patt 3[4].

Row 4 Moss st.

Cast off.

With RS facing place centre 12[14:8:20] sts on holder.

Knit across rem 15[16:18:21] sts.

Dec 1 st at neck edge on next and every foll alt row until 11[12:14:17]sts.

Cast off.

SHORT SLEEVES

Using 3.75mm (US5) needles and CC, cast on 36[42:42:48] sts.

Work 4 rows in moss stitch.

Change to MC and 4.75 (US7) needles and beg stripe sequence as for back at same time inc 1 st at each end of next and every foll alt row until 42[48:48:54] sts.

Work even until sleeve measures 2[2½:2½:3]in (5[6.5:6.5:8]cm), ending on a WS row.

Cast off.

LONG SLEEVES

Using 3.75mm (US5) needles and CC, cast on 30[36:36:42] sts.

Work 4 rows in moss stitch.

Change to 4.5mm (US7) needles and MC. Beg stripe sequence as for back at same time inc 1 st at each end of next and every foll 4th row until 42[48:48:54] sts.

Work even until sleeves measures 5[6½:7½:8½]in (13[16.5:19:22]cm), ending on a WS row.

Cast off.

LEFT CUFF

Using 3.75mm (US5) needles and CC, cast on 30[36:36:42] sts.

Work 4 rows in moss stitch.

Change to 4.5mm (US7) needles and MC. Beg stripe sequence as for back at same time inc 1 st at right edge on next and every foll 4th row until 34[40:40:46] sts.

Work even until cuff meas 3[3½:4:4]in (8[9:10:10]cm), ending on a WS. Change to CC and 3.75mm (US5) needles. Work 2 rows moss stitch.

Cast off.

RIGHT CUFF

Work as for left cuff but make increases on left edge instead.

POCKET

Using CC and 3.75mm (US5) needles, cast on 12 sts.

Moss st 4 rows.

Next row Moss st 2, k8, moss st 2.

Next row Moss st 2, p8, moss st 2.

Rep these 2 rows 8[10:12:12] times.

Decrease

Row 1 Moss 2, sl 1, k1, psso, k4, k2tog, moss st 2 (10 sts).

Row 2 Moss st 2, p6, moss st 2.

Row 3 Moss st 2, sl 1, k1, psso, k2, k2tog, moss st 2 (8 sts).

Row 4 Moss st 2, p4, moss st 2.

Row 5 Moss st 2, k2tog twice, moss st 2 (6 sts).

Row 6 Moss st 2, p2, moss st 2.

Row 7 Moss st 2, k2tog, moss st 2, (5 sts).

Cast off.

NECKBAND

Sew up right shoulder seam.

Using CC and 3.75mm (US5) needles and with RS facing, beg at front buttonhole band and PUK 8[10:12:12] sts down front of neck, knit across 12[14:18:20] sts from front stitch holder, 8[10:12:12] sts along second side of neck, 3 sts down back right shoulder, 18[20:24:26] sts from back stitch holder and 3 sts from left shoulder. 52[60:72:76] sts.

Moss st 3 rows.

Row 4 Buttonhole row: moss st 2, yo, k2tog, moss st to end.

Row 5 Moss st.

Cast off.

INTERIM MAKING UP

Sew all seams and darn in loose yarn ends.

Attach neck buttons and fasten.

LEG BANDS

Short version – back band

Using 3.75mm (US5) needles and CC, and with RS of back facing, PUK 34[40:52:64] sts.

Moss stitch 5 rows.

Cast off.

Long version – back band

Using 3.75mm (US5) needles and CC and with RS of back facing PUK 64[88:100:114] sts.

Moss stitch 5 rows.

Cast off.

Short version – front buttonhole band

PUK stitches as for back band.

Moss st 3 rows.

Buttonhole row

1st size only Patt 2, yo, k2tog *(k12, yo, k2tog) rep from * to last 2 sts, patt 2.

2nd and 3rd sizes Patt1, yo, k2tog *(k7[10], yo, k2tog) rep from * to last st, patt 1.

4th size Patt 3, yo, k2 tog *(k8, yo, k2tog) rep from * to last 3 sts, patt 3.

Moss st 1 row.

Cast off.

Long version – front buttonhole band

PUK stitches as for back band.

Moss st 3 rows.

Buttonhole row

1st, 2nd and 3rd sizes Patt 3, yo, k2tog *(k8, yo, k2tog) rep from * until last 3 sts, patt 3.

4th size Patt 1, yo, k2tog *(k10, yo, k2tog) rep from * until last st, patt 1.

Moss st 1 row.

Cast off.

FINAL MAKING UP

Mark position of buttons and sew in place. Position front pocket and sew in place. Pin and sew short sleeves in place. Sew up side seams.

For long sleeves fold right sleeve in half lengthwise. Place cuff with WS facing outwards on the outer part of sleeve. Slip stitch the sides and moss stitch band to the sleeve, leaving the upper edge open. Repeat for left sleeve. Pin and sew sleeves to romper. Sew as usual. Sew side seams.

alpaca moo hat & mittens

This quirky cow-print hat and mittens set are sure to attract attention and will be a huge hit with parents and babies alike. Why not knit the cow comforter (on page 76) to continue the fun animal theme?

Sizes

	0–3 months	3–6 months	6–12 months
To fit head circumference	12in	14in	18in
	30.5cm	36cm	46cm
Hat height	5½in	6in	7in
	14cm	15cm	18cm

Materials

Artesano Alpaca Inca Cloud 100%
Aplaca (120m/131yd per 50g ball)
2 x 50g balls in Cream
1 x 50g ball in Charcoal
1 x 50g ball in Baby Pink
3.25mm (US3)
4mm (US6) needles

Tension

25 sts x 33 rows over 4in (10cm)

Moo hat

Using 3.75mm (US3) needles and
Charcoal, cast on 72[80:104] sts.
Change to Cream and beg double
rib as follows:
Row 1 *(K2, p2) rep from * to end.
Rep this row for 6 rows.
Change to 4mm (US6) needles
and work chart patt (on page 74)
according to your size.
Shape crown
Using Cream.
Row 1 K2tog to end of row
36[40:52] sts.
Row 2 Purl.
Row 3 K2tog to end of row
18[20:26] sts.
Row 4 Purl.

Row 5 K2tog to end of row 9[10:13] sts.
Row 6 K1[0:1], k2 tog to end of row 5[5:7] sts.
Break yarn, leaving a long tail, thread through rem sts and pull tight.

INSIDE EARS (make 2 alike)
Using 3.25mm (US3) needles and Baby Pink, cast on 11 sts.
Row 1 *(K1, p1) rep from* to end of row.
Rep this row until ear measures 1½in (4cm).
Next row Keeping to moss st patt, k2tog at each end of row (9 sts).
Next row Moss st.
Rep these two rows until 3 sts.
Next row K3tog.
Break yarn, leaving a tail, thread through rem sts and pull tight.

OUTER EARS (make 2 alike)
Using 3.25mm (US3) needles and Cream, cast on 11 sts.
Beg with a knit row, work even in st st until ear measures 1½in (4cm), ending on a purl row.
Next row Dec 1 st at each end of row.
Next row Purl.
Rep these two rows until 3 sts rem.
Next row K3tog.
Break yarn, leaving a tail, thread through rem sts and pull tight.

MAKING UP
Ears
Darn in loose yarn ends. Place right sides of outer and inner ear together and sew around edge. Leave bottom seam open. Turn RS out and, using long yarn tail, do running stitches through the bottom seam and gather slightly. Repeat for second ear.
Hat
Press hat lightly. Sew rear seam. Position ears to side of head and pin in place. Sew in position using firm, neat stitches.

Mittens
(make 2 alike)
Using 3.25mm (US3) needles and Charcoal, cast on 28[32:34] sts.
Change to Cream and work single rib as follows:
Row 1 *k1, p1 rep from * to end
Work rib for 1[1:1½]in (2.5[2.5:4]cm).
Change to 4mm (US6) needles and work chart patt (on page 75) according to size.
Shape top
Using Cream.
Next row (SI 1, k1, psso, k10[12:13], k2tog) rep bracket seq twice 24[28:30] sts.
Next and every alt row Purl.
Next row *(SI 1, k1, psso, k8[10:11], k2tog) rep from * twice 20[24:26] sts.

Next row *(SI 1, k1, psso, k6[8:9], k2tog) rep from * twice 16[20:22] sts.
Next row Purl.
1st size only Cast off.
2nd and 3rd sizes
Next row (sl 1, k1, psso, k6(7), k2tog) rep bracket seq twice 16[18] sts.
Next row Purl.
Cast off.

MAKING UP
Press lightly and sew top and rear seam.
String
Using 6 strands of charcoal, make a plaited string 26[28:32]in (66[71:81]cm) long. Knot each end to secure.
Sew the ends of the tie firmly inside the cuff of each mitt.

Hat chart   36 sts x 38 rows [40 sts x 42 rows: 52 sts x 50 rows]

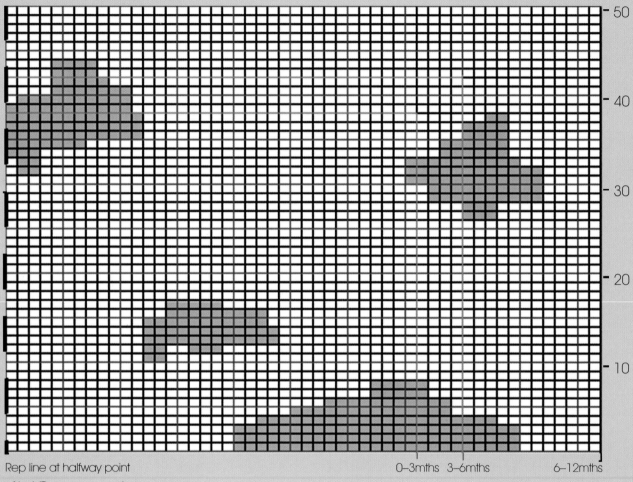

- 50

- 40

- 30

- 20

- 10

Rep line at halfway point
of hat (Rep once more)

0–3mths   3–6mths   6–12mths

Mittens chart   28 sts x 20 rows [32 sts x 24 rows: 34 sts x 24 rows]

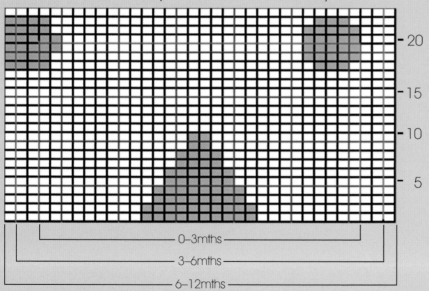

— 20

— 15

— 10

— 5

0–3mths
3–6mths
6–12mths

KEY
 Cream
Charcoal

Each square = 1 st and 1 row
Read RS rows (knit) from R to L and WS
rows (purl) from L to R.

alpaca comfort blankies

Many babies use blankies or comforters to soothe them to sleep. These ones have been designed with two vital things in mind: softness and strokeability. The alpaca yarn is beautifully huggable whilst satin ribbons make them soothing to the touch.

Size

Base comforter measures 12 x 12in (30.5 x 30.5cm)

Materials

SHEEP
Artesano Alpaca Inca Cloud 100% Alpaca (120m/131yd per 50g ball)
2 x 50g balls in Cream
1 x 50g ball in Charcoal
Cornish Organic Stuffing
1.5yd (1.5m) x 2in (5cm) wide satin ribbon
Small amount of white felt
Black embroidery thread

COW
Artesano Alpaca:
2 x 50g balls in Cream
1 x 50g ball in Charcoal
1 x 50g ball in Baby Pink
Cornish Organic Stuffing
1.5yd (1.5m) x 1 in (2.5cm) wide black and white speckled ribbon
Small amount of white felt
Black embroidery thread
3.5mm (US4) needles

Tension

25sts x 33 rows over 4in (10cm)

Base comforter

(for both cow and sheep)
Using 3.5mm needles and Cream, cast on 75 sts.
Beg with a knit row, work straight in st st until comforter measures 12in (30.5cm), ending on a WS row.
Cast off.
Pin and block the square.

Sheep head

Using Charcoal and 3.5mm needles, cast on 6 sts.
Row 1 Kfb into each st (12 sts)
Row 2 Purl
Row 3 *K1, kfb rep from * to end (18 sts).
Row 4 Purl.
St st 6 rows.
Next row *K2, kfb rep from * to end (24 sts).
Beg with a purl row, st st 3 rows.
Next row *K2, kfb rep from * to end

(32 sts)**.

Beg with a purl row, st st 9 rows.

Shape muzzle

Next row K2 tog to end of row (16 sts).

Next row Purl.

Next row K2tog to end of row (8 sts).

Next row Purl.

Next row K2 tog to end of row (4 sts).

Break yarn, leaving a long tail. Thread through rem sts and pull tight.

Fold head in half lengthwise and sew rear seam leaving a small opening. Stuff firmly and close hole.

EARS (make 2 alike)

Using Charcoal, cast on 5 sts.

Row 1 *K1, p1 rep from * to last st, k1.

Rep this row six times.

Next row K2tog, moss st to last 2 sts, k2tog (3 sts).

Break yarn, leaving a long tail, thread through rem sts and pull tight.

Position ears at each side of head and sew firmly in place (see photo for reference).

Cow head

Using 3.5mm needles and Cream, work as for sheep to **.

Next row Beg with a purl row, work 5 rows in st st.

Change to Baby Pink and work 4 rows in st st.

Work muzzle decreases as for sheep's head.

Work both ears as for sheep, using Cream.

Stuff and attach ears as for sheep.

Making up

Pin and tack ribbon around the edges of the base comforters.

You will need to mitre the corners for neatness. The wide satin ribbon should be folded lengthwise over each side edge, whilst the narrower black and white ribbon can sit on top of the right side. Sew firmly in place using small slip stitches.

SHEEP

Cut two small circles of white felt for eyes. Position and secure in the centre with a French knot, worked in black embroidery thread (see page 138 for instructions). Work two more French knots on muzzle for nostrils.

Take some of the Cream yarn and work French knots all over the crown of the sheep so it looks like wool. Don't be too fussy and leave some knots a bit loopy to add texture.

COW

Work eyes and nostrils as for the sheep. Take some of the Charcoal yarn and Swiss darn a small, random area on the cow's face so it looks like a Friesian. Add more patches if you like. Go on, personalize your cow! (See page 138 for swiss darning instructions.)

RIBBON HANDLES

Fold your base comforters in half and then in half again to find the centre point.

Cut an 8in (20cm) length of ribbon. Fold in half and lay the raw edges on the centre point of the base. Secure the ribbon in place with small firm stitches.

Place your sheep or cow head over the top and secure to the ribbon/base comforter with small, firm stitches.

PART TWO

Toddlers

(1-3 years)

corn fibre lace pyjamas

These classic lace pyjamas are soft and comfy for a good night's sleep. The leggings are three-quarter length and trimmed with lace and ribbon which is echoed in the empire-line top. So pretty, they could even be used for daywear!

Sizes

	6–12 months	1–2 years	2–3 years
PYJAMA BOTTOMS			
Finished waist	20in	22in	24in
	51cm	56cm	61cm
Total length	11in	12in	14in
	28cm	30.5cm	36cm
PYJAMA TOP			
Actual chest	22in	24in	26in
	56cm	61cm	66cm
Finished length	13in	15in	16in
	33cm	38cm	41cm

Materials

SWTC Amaizing 100% Corn fibre
(130m/142yds per 50g ball)
5[5:6] x 50g balls in shade Cream Puff
3m of narrow burgundy ribbon
Stitch holders
Elastic for waistbands
4 x pearl buttons
3.75 (US5) needles
4.5mm (US7) needles

Tension

6 sts x 8 rows over 4in (10cm)

Pyjama bottoms

FRONT AND BACK

(make 2 pieces alike)
Using 3.75mm (US5) needles, cast on 60[66:72] sts
Casing Beg with a k row, st st 5 rows. Turning row, knit.
Change to 4.5mm (US7) needles and beg with a knit row, st st for another 7[7:8]in (18[18:20.5]cm), ending on a WS row.
Divide for legs
Next row K27[30:33], turn. Work on these sts only. Leave rem sts on holder.

Work in st st for a further 4[5:6]in (10[13:15]cm) ending, on a purl row. Cast off.

Second leg

With RS facing, rejoin yarn to rem 33[36:39] sts.

Cast off 6 sts. 27[30:33] sts.

Work even in st st to match first leg. Cast off.

MAKING UP

Sew side seams of bottoms. Fold down waistband casing to WS of trousers. Pin and slip stitch in place leaving a small opening for elastic. Attach elastic to a safety pin and feed through casing. Adjust to correct size: sew ends of elastic firmly and close opening. Using 3.75mm (US5) needles work lace edging (see box for instructions), so it fits around the bottom edge of first leg. Cast off. Sew neatly in place. Rep for second leg.

Using a large-eyed needle, thread ribbon through eyelet holes in the lace edging. Snip to correct length and secure ribbon ends with a few stitches along inside leg seam.

Pyjama top

FRONT

*Using 4.5mm (US7) needles cast on 84[90:96] sts.

Work 4 rows in st st.

Row 5 K2, sl1, k1, psso, knit to last 4 sts, k2tog, k2.

Rep this dec row on every foll 6th row until 66[72:78] sts.

Work even in st st until skirt measures 7[7½:8]in (18[19:20.5]cm), ending on a knit row.

Next row Knit.

Beg with a knit row, work even for a further 2in (5cm) ending, on a purl row.

lace edging

Using 3.75mm (US5) needles cast on 4 sts.

Knit 1 row.

Row 1 K2, yf, k2.

Rows 2, 4 and 6 Knit.

Row 3 K3, yf, k2.

Row 5 K2, yf, k2tog, yf, k2.

Row 7 K3, yf, k2tog, yf, k2.

Row 8 Cast off 4 sts, knit to end.

Rep these 8 rows for length required, casting off on a pattern row.

Shape armholes

Cast off 6 sts at beg of next 2 rows,
54[60:66] sts**.

Dec 1 st at neck edge on next and foll
alt rows until 38[40:42] sts, ending on a
purl row.

Shape neck

K12[11:11] sts turn and work on
these sts.

Dec 1 st at neck edge on next and foll
alt rows until 8 sts.

Work even until front measures
12[14:15]in (30.5[36:38]cm), ending
on a WS row.

Cast off.

Second side

With RS facing, slip centre 14[18:20] sts
on holder.

Rejoin yarn to rem 12[11:11] sts and
work as for first side, reversing shapings.

BACK

Work as for front from * to **.

Dec 1 st at each end of next and
every foll alt row until 48[50:52] sts,
ending on a purl row.

Divide for back opening

Next row K2tog, k22[23:24] sts, turn.
Leave rem 24[25:26] sts on holder.

Next row Cast on 3 sts, knit them, purl
to end 25[26:30] sts.

Next row K2tog, knit to end 24[25:29]
sts.

Next row K3, purl to end.
Rep the last 2 rows until 22[23:24] sts
rem, ending on a purl row.

Next row K12[11:11] sts. Leave rem
10[12:13] sts on holder.
Turn, purl to end.

Shape shoulders

Dec 1 st at neck edge on next and foll
alt rows until 8 sts rem.

Work to even in st st to match front.

Cast off.

Second side

With RS facing, rejoin yarn to rem st.

Next row Knit to last 2 sts, k2tog
23[24:25] sts.

Next row Purl to last 3 sts, k3.
Rep last 2 rows until 19[20:21] sts,
ending on purl row.

Next row k7[9:10] sts. Slip these st onto
holder, knit to last 2 sts, k2tog 11[10:10]
sts.

Next row Purl.

Dec 1 st at neck edge on next and foll
alt rows until 8 sts rem.

Work even in st st to match first side.

Cast off.

ARMBANDS

Sew shoulder seams.

Using 3.75mm (US5) needles PUK
48[54:60] sts along first armhole edge.

Garter st 3 rows.

Cast off.

Rep for second side.

NECKBAND

With RS of back facing and using
3.75mm (US5) needles knit across
7[9:10] sts from right back holder, 12
up right shoulder, 12 sts down right
front, 14[18:20] sts from front holder, 12
sts up left front shoulder, 12 sts down
left back shoulder and 10[12:12] sts
from back holder, 79[87:90] sts.
Next row Knit.
Next row Buttonhole row, k3, yf, k2tog,
knit to end.
Garter st for another row.
Cast off loosely.

MAKING UP

Darn in loose yarn ends. Join side
seams. Sew 3 pearl buttons on centre
front, above the waistline. Sew button
on rear opening. Tuck button flap inside
opening and secure with a few neat
stitches. Knit lace edging to fit around
lower end of skirt (see box on page
81 for instructions). Sew in place and,
using a large-eyed needle, thread
ribbon through lace eyelets. Snip to
correct length. Secure ribbon ends at
inside edge of side seam.

corn fibre hooded gilet

A fun and practical gilet to throw over t-shirts and jumpers for a bit of extra warmth. The bi-coloured rib is bright and cheery making it sure to become a firm favourite with parents and toddlers.

Sizes

	0–6 months	6–12 months	1–2 years	2–3 years
Finished chest	22in	24in	27in	29in
	56cm	61cm	69cm	74cm
Length from shoulder	10in	12in	13in	14in
	25.5cm	30.5cm	33cm	36cm

Materials

SWTC Amaizing 100% Corn fibre
(130m/142yd per 50g ball)
4[4:5:5] x 50g balls in shade 363
Atlantis (MC).
1[1:1:1] x 50g balls in shade 366
Grenadine (CC).
8[10:12:12]in (20.5[25.5:30.5:30.5]cm)
Open-ended zip in blue
3.75 (US5) needles
4.5mm (US7) needles
2 x stitch markers
3 x stitch holders

Tension

24 sts x 32 rows over 4in (10cm)

Gilet

BACK

Using 3.75mm (US5) needles and MC,
cast on 64[72:80:88] sts.

Beg coloured rib as follows

Row 1 P1 in MC *k2 in CC, P2 in MC
rep from * until last st, p1 in MC.

Row 2 K1 in MC (p2 in CC, k2 in MC)
rep from * until last st, k1 in MC.

Rep last 2 rows until rib measures
1[1:1½:1½]in (2.5[2.5:4:4]cm), ending
on row 2.

Break CC.

Change to 4.5mm (US7) needles
and work even in MC in st st until work
measures 6[7½:8½:9]in
(15[19:22:23]cm), ending on a purl row.

Shape armholes

Cast off 6 sts at beg of next 2 rows.

52[60:68:76] sts.

Work even in st st until back measures 10[12:13:14]in (25.5[30.5:33:36]cm), ending on purl row

Shape shoulders

Next row K16[18:21:24], turn.

Work on these sts only.

Next row P2tog, purl to end 15[17:20:23] sts.

Slip centre 20[24:26:28] sts onto holder. Rejoin yarn to second side.

Next row Knit across 16[18:21:24] sts.

Next row Purl to last 2 sts, p2tog. Cast off.

LEFT FRONT

*Using MC and 3.75mm (US5) needles, cast on 32[36:40:44] sts.

Work coloured rib as for back.**

Change to 4.5mm (US7) needles and work in MC as follows:

Row 1 Knit.

Row 2 K2, purl to end.

Rep row 1 and 2 until work measures 2[2½:3:3]in (5[6.5:8:8]cm), ending on a purl row.

Pocket

K12[14:15:16] sts, turn. Leave rem 20[22:25:28] sts on holder.

Cast on 15[15:18:20] sts (optional, you can use CC here if you want a coloured pocket lining), purl to end, 27[29:33:36] sts.

Work 23 rows even in st st ending, with a knit row.

Next row Cast off 15[15:18:20] sts.

Leave rem 12[14:15:16] sts on holder.

With RS facing, rejoin yarn to rem 20[22:25:28] sts.

Beg with a knit row, work 23 rows in st st, ending on a knit row.

Next row K2, p18[20:23:26], purl across 12[14:15:16] sts from holder. 32[36:40:44] sts.

Cont working row 1 and 2 as before until work measures 6[7½:8½:9]in (15[19:22:23]cm), ending on a purl row.

Shape armholes

Cast off 6 sts at beg of next row 26[30:34:38] sts.

Work row 1 and 2 until work measures 12 rows less than back, ending on row 1

Shape neck

Next row Cast off 4 sts, purl to end. 22[26:30:34] sts.

Next row Knit. Place marker at neck edge.

Next row Cast off 2[2:2:3] sts at neck edge, purl to end. 20[24:28:31] sts.

Next and alt rows Knit.

Next row Cast off 2[2:2:2] sts at neck edge, purl to end 18[22:26:29] sts.

Next row Cast off 1[2:2:2] sts at neck edge, purl to end 17[20:24:27] sts.

Next row Cast off 1[2:2:2] sts at neck edge, purl to end 16[18:22:25] sts.

Next row Cast off 1[1:2:2] sts at neck edge, purl to end 15[17:20:23] sts.

Cast off.

RIGHT FRONT

Work as for left front from * to **.
Change to 4.5mm (US7) needles and
work in MC as follows:

Row 1 Knit.

Row 2 Purl to last 2 sts, k2.

Rep rows 1 and 2 until work measures
2[2½:3:3]in (5[6.5:8:8]cm), ending on
a purl row.

Pocket

Next row K20[22:25:28] sts, turn. Leave
rem 12[14:15:16] sts on holder.

Next row Purl to last 2 sts, k2.

Next row Knit.

Rep last 2 rows for 24 rows, ending on
knit row. Break yarn. Leave sts on holder.

With RS facing Cast on 15[15:18:20]
sts (again, use CC for contrast lining),
knit across rem 12[14:15:16] sts from
first holder. 27[29:33:36] sts.

Next row Work 23 rows in st st ending
on a purl row.

Next row Cast off 15[15:18:20] sts, knit
to end, 12[14:15:16] sts.

Next row P12[14:15:16] sts,
p18[20:23:26] sts from holder, k2.
32[36:40:44] sts.

Work rows 1 and 2 until work measures
6[7½:8½:9]in (15[19:22:23]cm),
ending on row 1.

Shape armhole

Cast off 6 sts at beg of next row, purl to
last 2 sts, k2. 26[30:34:38] sts.

Work remainder sts for left front,
reversing neck shaping sts.

INTERIM MAKE-UP

Sew shoulder seams. Darn in loose
yarn ends. Pin and slip stitch pocket
lining to WS of each front.

POCKET TOP

With RS facing, 3.75mm (US5) needles
and MC, PUK 20 sts along pocket
edge.

Work row 2 and row 1 of coloured rib.

Work row 2 once more.

Cast off.

Sew in loose ends and slip stitch short
ends of bands neatly in place.

Rep for second pocket.

ARMBAND

With RS facing, 3.75mm (US5) needles
and MC PUK 48[56:60:60] sts along first
armhole.

Work row 2 of coloured rib.

Work row 1 and 2, twice.

Cast off.

Rep for second side.

Darn in loose yarn ends and sew side
seams.

HOOD

With RS facing, 4.5mm (US7) needles and MC, PUK 16 sts along right front from marker, 3 sts from right back, 20[24:26:28] sts from centre back holder, 3 sts from left back and 16 sts down left front to marker.
58[62:64:66] sts.

Beg with knit row, work 3 rows st st.

Next row K27[29:30:31] m1, k4, m1, k27[29:30:31]. 60[64:66:68] sts.

Next row Beg with a purl row, st st 5 rows.

Next row K27[29:30:31], m1, k6, m1 k27[29:30:31]. 62[66:68:70] sts.

Next row Beg with purl row, st st 5 rows.

Next row K27[29:30:31], m1, k8, m1, k27[29:30:31]. 64[68:70:72] sts.

Cont inc in this way on every 6th row until 68[74:78:82] sts.

Work 11[11:11:17] rows even in st st.

Dec as follows:

Next row K31[34:36:38], s11, k1, psso, k2, k2tog, k31[34:36:38]. 66[72:76:80] sts.

Next and alt rows Purl.

Next row K30[33:35:37], sl1, k1, psso, k2, k2tog k30[33:35:37]. 64[70:74:78] sts.

Next row K29[32:34:36], sl1, k1, psso, k2, k2tog, k29[32:34:36]. 62[68:72:76] sts.

Rep dec rows as set until 58[62:64:66] sts, ending on purl row.

Cast off.

MAKING UP

Sew hood seam and darn in loose yarn ends.

Hood band

With RS facing, 3.75mm (US5) needles and MC PUK 64[76:88:112] sts around hood edge.

Work row 2 of coloured rib.

Work rows 1 and 2, twice.

Cast off.

Sew in loose ends and sew bottom ends of band to front edges of gilet.

Pin and sew zip in place.

knitknack

This yarn comes in an array of bright and pretty colours. Try coming up with your own colourways. Pinks and purples would be great for girls.

wool cable jumper & earflap hat

A fun jumper in a rainbow of colours that your toddler will love to wear when out and about. Inside-out seams and no fiddly stitches to pick up around the neck make this jumper perfect for those who don't like the finishing-off bits!

Sizes

	6–12 months	1–2 years	2–3 years
Finished chest	24in	26in	28in
	61cm	66cm	71cm
Length from shoulder	12in	14in	15in
	30.5cm	36cm	38cm
Sleeve length	8in	9in	10in
	20.5cm	23cm	25.5cm
Hat circumference	16in	17in	18in
	41cm	43cm	46cm

Materials

SWTC Karoake 50% soy silk, 50% Wool
(100m/109yd per 50g ball)
JUMPER
3[3:4] x 50g balls in Playful (shade 297)
EARFLAP HAT
1 x 50g ball of Playful
4.5mm (US7) needles
2 x stitch holders
Cable needle
3.5mm (USE/4) crochet hook

Tension

20 sts x 24 rows per 4 inch (10cm)

Cable jumper

FRONT AND BACK
(make 2 pieces alike)
Using 4.5mm (US7) needles, cast on
60[66:70] sts.
Row 1 (RS) p24[27:29] k12, p24[27:29].
Row 2 K24[27:29)] p12, k24[27:29].
Rep rows 1 & 2 twice more.
Row 7 P24[27:29] C6F, C6B,
p24[27:29].
Row 8 As row 2.
Rep these 8 rows until work measures
7[8:9]in (18[20.5:23]cm), ending on a
WS row.
Shape raglan
Keeping to cable patt, cast off 3 sts at

beg of next 2 rows 54[60:64] sts.
Dec 1 st at each end of next and foll
alt rows until 20[24:26] sts rem, ending
on WS row.
Cast off.

SLEEVES

Using 4.5mm (US7) needles, cast on
30[34:36] sts.
Row 1 (RS) p9[10:12], k12, p9[10:12].
Row 2 K9[10:12], p12, k9[10:12].
Rep these 2 rows twice more.
Row 7 P9[10:12] C6F, C6B, p9[10:12]].
Row 8 As row 2.
Work cable patt as set at same
time inc 1 st at each end of 3rd row
and then every alt [4th:4th] row until
60[66:70] sts.
Work even until sleeve measures
8[9:10]in (20.5[23:25.5]cm), ending on
a WS row.
Shape raglan
Keeping to cable patt, cast off 3 sts at
beg of next 2 rows 54[60:64] sts.
Dec 1 st at each end of next and foll
alt rows until 20[24:26] sts rem.
Cast off.

MAKING UP

Darn in loose yarn ends. Press lightly.
With WS together, pin and sew raglans
in place with back stitch so raw seams
show on the outside of the garment.
Turn inside out. Pin and sew sleeve and
side seams. Turn RS out.

Earflap hat

EARFLAPS

(make 2)
Using 4.5mm (US7) needles, cast on
2 sts.
K2 rows.
Next row Kfb twice (4 sts).
K4 rows.
Inc row Kfb, knit to last st, kfb (6 sts).
K4 rows.
Inc row Kfb, knit to last st, kfb (8 sts).
K4 rows.
Keep inc on every 5th row until 20 sts.
Work even in garter stitch until flap
measures 5in (13cm).
Break yarn and leave flap on stitch
holder.

HAT

Cast on 11[12:13] sts, knit 20 sts from
first earflap, cast on 22[24:26] sts, knit
20 sts from second earflap, cast on
11[12:13] sts (84[88:92] sts).
Next row Knit.
Row 1 (RS) P36[38:40], k12, p36[38:40].
Row 2 K36[38:40], p12, k36[38:40].
Rep rows 1 and 2, 3 times (6 rows in
total).
Row 7 P36[38:40], C6F, C6B,
p36[38:40].
Rep these 7 rows until hat meas 5[6:7]
in (13[15:18]cm), ending on a WS row.
Dec for crown
Row 1 K2 tog to end 42[44:46] sts.
Rep row 1, 21[22:23] sts.

Next row K1[0:1], k2tog to end,
11[11:12] sts.
Break yarn, thread through rem st
and pull tight.

MAKING UP

Darn in loose yarn ends. Press lightly.
Sew rear hat seam. Make 3 pompoms
(see page 137 for instructions). Sew
one to the top of the hat and one on
end of both earflaps. Double crochet
one round evenly around outer edge
of hat ie. earflaps, lower front and back
edges. (See page 139 for instructions.)

hemp t-shirt & combat pants

Combat pants are a brilliant choice for active toddlers. This version is knitted in hemp which is durable and comfortable – perfect for hours of climbing and sliding in the park. The matching loose-fit t-shirt completes a great play outfit.

Sizes

	6–12 months	1–2 years	2–3 years
COMBAT PANTS			
Waist	22in	24in	27in
	56cm	61cm	69cm
Total length	16½in	18in	20in
	42cm	46cm	51cm
Inside leg	9½in	10½in	12in
	24cm	27cm	30.5cm
T-SHIRT			
Finished chest	24in	26in	28in
	61cm	66cm	71cm
Length from shoulder	11in	13in	15in
	28cm	33cm	38cm

Materials

House of Hemp 4-ply
(85m/93yd per 50g skein)
COMBAT PANTS
3[4:4] x 50g skeins in Huff
2 buttons (by Stockwell Pottery, see *Stockists*, page 142)
Elastic for waist
T-SHIRT
2[3:3] x 50g skeins Huff
2[2:3] x 50g skeins Wow

3 buttons (as for combat pants)
4 stitch holders
3.5mm (US4) and 4mm (US6) needles

Tension

20 sts x 30 rows over 4in (10cm)

Combat pants

LEGS

(make 2)

Casing Using Huff and 3.5mm (US4) needles, cast on 56[60:68] sts

Beg with a knit row, st st 5 rows, ending in a knit row.

Next (turning) row Knit.

Next row Work 6 rows garter stitch.

Change to 4mm (US6) needles and work even in st st for a further 7[7½:8½]in (18[19:22]cm), ending on a purl row.

Dec 1 st at each end of next and every foll alt row until 50[56:60] sts.

Work even in st st until work measures 15½[17:19]in (39.5[43:48.5]cm), ending on a purl row.

Cuff

Change to 3.5mm (US4) needles and work 8 rows in garter stitch.

Beg with a knit row, work 6 rows in stocking stitch.

Cast off.

POCKETS

(make 2)

Using 4mm (US6) needles, cast on 20 sts.

Work even in st st until pocket measures 3½in (9cm), ending on a purl row.

Garter st 2 rows.

Buttonhole row K3, cast off 2 sts, k10, cast off 2 sts, k3.

Next row K3, cast off 2 sts, k10, cast off 2 sts, k3.

Work 2 more rows in garter stitch.

Cast off.

MAKING UP

Pin and block pieces into shape. Darn in loose yarn ends. Join front and back crotch seams. Sew side and inside leg seams.

Fold down waistband casing to WS of pants. Pin and slip stitch into place, leaving a small opening for threading elastic. Attach the length of elastic to a safety pin and feed through casing. Adjust to correct size. Sew elastic ends firmly and close opening.

Fold bottom cuffs up to WS side of trouser leg. Slip stitch in place leaving a small opening. Feed elastic through as for waistband and adjust to ankle size. Sew elastic firmly and close opening. Rep for second leg cuff.

Position pocket on outside of leg, just below the crotch line. Pin and sew in place.

Mark position of buttons and sew firmly in place. Button up pocket.

Rep for second pocket.

T-shirt

BACK

*Using 3.5mm (US4) needles and Wow, cast on 60[66:70] sts.

Garter st for 6 rows.

Change to 4mm (US6) needles and Huff. Beg with a knit row, work even in stocking stitch and following stripe patt throughout:

2 rows Huff

6 rows Wow

Work even until 6½[8:9]in (16.5[20.5:23]cm), ending on a purl row. **

Shape armholes

Cast off 3 sts at beg of next 2 rows. 54[60:64] sts.

Dec 1 st at each end of next and foll alt rows until 18[20:20] sts, ending on a purl row.

Leave sts on holder.

FRONT

Work as for back from * to **.

Shape armholes

Cast off 8 sts at beg of next row 52[58:62] sts.

Next row Cast off 3 sts at beg of next row 49[55:59] sts.

Dec 1 st at each end of next and foll alt rows until 13[15:15] sts, ending on a purl row.

Leave sts on holder.

SLEEVES

(make 2)

Using 3.5mm (US4) needles and Huff, cast on 40[46:52] sts.

Garter st 6 rows.

Change to 4mm (US6) needles

Inc 1 st at each end of next and foll alt rows until 54[56:64] sts.

Work even until sleeve measures 3in (8cm), ending on a purl row.

Shape armholes

Cast off 3 sts at beg of next 2 rows 48[50:64] sts.

Dec 1 st at each end of next and foll alt rows until 10[12:14] sts.

Leave sts on holder.

LEFT FRONT BUTTON BAND

Pin and block front.

Darn in loose yarn ends.

With RS facing and using 3.5mm (US4) and Huff, PUK 34[34:40] sts along left front raglan.

Row 1 *K1, p1 rep from * to end.

Row 2 Buttonhole row (P1, k1) 7[7:10] times, cast off 2 sts, (p1, k1)4 times, cast off 2 sts, (p1, k1) 4 times

Row 3 (K1, p1) 4 times, cast on 2 sts, (k1, p1)4 times, cast on 2 sts, (k1, p1) 7[7:10] times.

Row 4 *P1, k1 rep from * to end.

Row 5 As row 1.

Cast off.

SLEEVE BUTTON BAND

Pin and block one of the sleeves.
Darn in loose yarn ends.
With RS facing and using 3.5mm (US4)
needles and Huff, PUK 34[34:40] sts
along left side of sleeve raglan.
Rib for 3 rows.
Cast off.

NECKBAND

Pin and block back and second
sleeve. Darn in loose yarn ends.
Pin and sew both back raglan
seams. Sew front right raglan seam.
With RS facing and using 3.5mm
(US4) needles and Huff, PUK 3 sts
along the top of the right front button
band, 13[15:15] sts from front stitch
holder, 10[12:14] sts from right sleeve
holder, 18[20:20] sts from rear holder,
10[12:14] sts from left sleeve holder
and 2 sts from top of sleeve button
band. 56[64:68] sts.
Row 1 *K1, p1 rep from * to end.
Row 2 Buttonhole row P1, k1, cast off 2
sts, *p1, k1 rep from * to end.
Row 3 *K1, p1 rep from * to last 4 sts,
cast on 2 sts, k1, p1.
Rib 2 more rows.
Cast off loosely in rib.
Darn in all loose ends.
Sew buttons in place along the sleeve
button band. Fasten raglan.
Sew sleeve and side seams.

knitknack

Why not leave the elastic out of the
bottom cuffs of the combat pants
for a wider, looser fit? Hemp's
beautiful draping qualities would
lend itself wonderfully to this look.

alpaca cardigan & beret

Knitted in warm, soft alpaca, this cardigan has a slight flare to it. It is trimmed with a goblet hem, contrast colour cast-on edge and traditional, handworked Dorset buttons. The smart beret makes this a perfect outfit for special occasions.

Sizes

	0–6 months	6–12 months	1–2 years	2–3 years
CARDIGAN				
Chest	16in	18in	20in	22in
	41cm	46cm	51cm	56cm
Actual	20in	22in	24in	26in
	51cm	56cm	61cm	66cm
Sleeve seam	6in	7in	8in	10in
	15cm	18cm	20.5cm	25.5cm
Length from shoulder	9in	10in	11in	13in
	23cm	25.5cm	28cm	33cm
BERET				
Head circumference	14in	16in	17in	18in
	36cm	41cm	43cm	46cm

Materials

Artesano Inca Cloud 100% Alpaca
(120m/131yd per 50g ball)

CARDIGAN
1[1:1:1] x 50g ball in Oatmeal
3[4:4:5] x 50g balls in Chocolate

BERET
1[1:1:1] x 50g ball in Oatmeal
1[1:1:1] x 50g ball in Chocolate

3.5mm (US4) needles
4mm (US6) needles
2 Prym – 10 x 22mm creative buttons
for Dorset Buttons
3 x stitch holders

Tension

25 sts x 33 rows over 4in (10cm)

Cardigan

BACK

Using 4mm (US6) needles and Oatmeal cast on 165[181:197:213] sts. Change to Chocolate.

Work ruffle as follows

Row 1 (WS) K5 *p11, k5 rep from * to end.

Row 2 P5 *k2tog, k7, ssk, p5 rep from * to end.

Row 3 K5 *p9, k5 from * to end.

Row 4 p5 *k2tog, k5, ssk, p5 from * to end.

Cont in this way, dec 1 st at each side of knit sts on every RS rows and working 2 purl sts less in each rep on every WS rows until 3 knit sts rem for each ruffle, ending with a WS row.

Next row P5 *sl2tog, k1, psso, p5 rep from * to end.

Next row K5 *p1, k5 rep from * to end.
**

Change to st st and beg with a knit row, dec 3[3:1:1] sts evenly across next row. 64[68:76:82] sts.

Work even in st st until work measures 5[5½:6:8]in (32[14:15:20.5]cm), ending on a WS row.

Shape armhole

Cast off 4 sts at beg of next 2 rows. 56[60:68:74] sts.

Work even in st st until armhole measures 4[4½:5:5]in (10[11.5:13:13]cm), ending on a WS row.

Shape shoulders

Next row K19[19:22:23] sts, leave rem sts on holder.

Next row P2tog, purl to end of row 18[18:21:22] sts.

Cast off.

Leave middle 18[22:24:28] sts on holder.

Rejoin yarn and knit across rem 19[19:22:23] sts.

Next row Purl to last 2 sts, p2tog. 18[18:21:22] sts.

Cast off.

LEFT FRONT

Using 4mm (US6) needles and Oatmeal, cast on 85[85:101:101] sts. Change to Chocolate.

Work ruffle as for back until **.

Next row Knit, dec 3[1:3:0] sts evenly across this row. 32[34:38:41] sts.

Next row K6, purl to end.

Next row Knit.

Cont to work the last two rows until front matches the back at armhole level, ending on WS row.

Shape armholes

Cast off 4 sts on next row. 28[30:34:37] sts *.

Work even in patt until front measures 12[12:15:15] rows less than the back, ending on a WS

Next row Knit to last 6 sts. Put these 6 sts on holder.

Shape neck

Next row Purl.

Dec 1 st at neck edge on next and every foll row until 18[18:21:22] sts rem. Work even in st st until front matches the back.

Cast off.

RIGHT FRONT

Work as for left front, reversing all shapings to *.

Work even in patt until armhole measures 2[2½:3:3]in (5[6.5:8:8]cm), ending on a WS row.

Buttonhole row K2, cast off 3 sts, knit to end.

Next row Purl to last 6 sts, k1, cast off 3 sts, k2.

Work even in patt until front measures 12[12:15:15] rows less than back, ending on a WS row.

Work as for left front from ** to end, reversing all shapings.

SLEEVES

(make 2)

Using 3.5mm (US4) needles and Oatmeal, cast on 38[40:44:46] sts. Change to Chocolate and work 4 rows in garter stitch.

Change to 4mm (US6) needles.

Beg with a knit row, work even in st st at the same time inc 1 st at each edge of 3rd and every foll 6th row until 50[56:64:64] sts.

Cont to work even in st st until sleeve meas 6[7:8:10]in (15[18:20.5:25.5]cm), ending on a WS row.

Cast off.

NECKBAND

Join both shoulder seams.

With RS facing and using 3.5mm (US4) needles, knit across 6 sts from holder on right front, PUK 12[12:15:15] sts up right front edge, 2 sts across right back, knit across 18[22:24:28] sts from back stitch holder, 2 sts across left back, PUK 12[12:15:15] sts down left front edge, knit across 6 sts from holder on left front. 58[62:70:74] sts.

Garter stitch 2 rows.

Buttonhole row K2, Cast off 3 sts, knit to end.

Next row Knit to last 5 sts, cast off 3 sts, k2.

Next row Knit.

Cast off loosely.

MAKING UP

Darn in loose yarn ends and press pieces lightly. Pin and sew sleeves in place. Pin and sew side seams. Make the Dorset button (see box opposite for instructions) and sew in place on neckband.

Beret

Using 3.5mm (US4) needles and Oatmeal, cast on 88[100:104:112] sts.

Change to Chocolate.

Work 10 rows of k1, p1 rib.

Change to 4mm (US6) needles.

Increase as follows:

Row 1 (K3,kfb) rep to end of row 110[125:130:140] sts.

Row 2 Purl.

Beg with a knit row, work 4[6:8:10] rows in st st.

Increase as follows:

Next row *K4,kfb rep from * to end of row 132[150:156:168] sts

Next row Purl.

Beg with a knit row, work 2[4:6:8] rows in st st.

Dec for crown

Next row K4 *k2tog rep from * to end of row 110[125:130:140] sts.

Beg with a purl row, st st 3 rows.

Next row *K3, k2tog rep from * to end of row 88[100:104:112] sts.

Beg with a purl row, st st 3 rows.

Next row *K2, k2tog rep from * to end of row 66[75:78:84] sts.

Beg with a purl row, st st 3 rows.

Next row *K1, k2tog rep from * to end of row 44[50:52:56] sts.

Beg with a purl row, st st 3 rows.

Next row K2tog to end of row 22[25:26:28] sts.

Next row Purl.

Next row K0[1:0:0], *k2tog rep from * to end of row 11[13:13:14] sts

Next row P1[1:1:0], (p2tog) to end of row 6[7:7:7] sts.

Break yarn leaving a long tail. Thread through rem sts and pull tight.

Press beret lightly.

MAKING UP

Darn in loose yarn ends and sew rear seam. Make a Dorset button, as before, and sew onto front of beret over right eye.

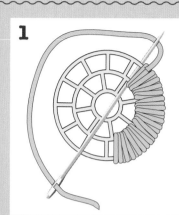

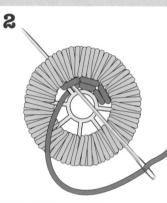

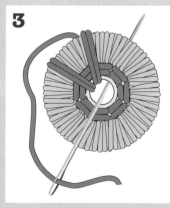

Dorset buttons

1 Using colour 1, work a round of vertical buttonhole stitches around the top two thirds of the button blank. Make sure every partition is generously filled before moving onto the next. Fasten off by darning a few stitches into the back of the button.

2 Using colour 2, work a round of back stitches through the holes nearest the centre of the blank. Travel clockwise and horizontally, working several stitches through each partition.

3 Now, still using colour 2, thread it through the centre hole and wind up over the top edge of the button. Wrap twice for a bold stripe. Repeat this at twelve o'clock, 5 past, quarter past, 20 past, half past etc until you have a wheel-like effect. Fasten off by darning a few stitches into the back of the button.

wool aran cable jumper

This oversized aran sweater is so easy to knit and wonderful to throw on over your toddler's jeans. For breezy days rockpooling along the shoreline or kicking leaves in country lanes, this sweater is perfect for minimizing cold and maximizing fun!

Sizes

	1–2 years		2–3 years	
Finished chest	26in	66cm	30in	76cm
Length from shoulder	13in	33cm	15in	38cm
Sleeve length	9in	23cm	10in	25.5cm

Materials

Cornish Organic Aran Wool
(225m/246yd per 100g skein)
3[3] x 100g skeins
4.5mm (US7) needles
5mm (US8) needles
Cable needle
Stitch holders

Tension

20 sts x 24 rows over 4in (10cm) over cable patt

SPECIAL ABBREVIATION
C6B Slip next 3 sts onto cable needle and hold to back of work, k3, slip 3 sts from cable needle onto left-hand needle and knit.

Jumper

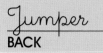

BACK

Using 4.5mm (US7) needles, cast on
64[76] sts.

Beg with a knit row, st st 4 rows.

Next row *K2, p2 rep from * to end.

Next row *P2, k2 rep from * to end.

Rep this double rib row for 6[5] rows.

2nd size only

Inc 1 st at each end of next row (78 sts).

All sizes

Change to 5mm (US8) needles and
beg cable patt as follows:

1st size

Row 1 K2, p2, k12 *p2, k6, p2, k12 rep
from * to last 4 sts, p2, k2.

Row 2 P2, k2, p12 *k2, p6, k2, p12 rep
from * to last 4 sts, k2, p2.

Rep rows 1 and 2 twice more.

Row 7 K2, p2, k12 *p2, C6B, p2, k12
rep from * to last 4 sts, p2, k2.

Row 8 As row 2.

Rows 9 and 10 As rows 1 and 2.

Row 11 K5, p2, k6, p2, *k12, p2, k6,
p2 rep from * to last 5 sts, k5.

Row 12 P5, k2, p6, k2 *p12, k2, p6, k2
rep from * to last 5 sts, p5.

Rep rows 11 & 12 twice more.

Row 17 K5, p2, C6B, p2 *k12, p2, C6B,
p2 rep from * to last 5 sts, k5.

Row 18 As row 11.

Rows 19 and 20 As rows 11 and 12.

2nd size

Row 1 K1*p2, k6, p2, k12 rep from * to
last 11 sts, p2, k6, p2, k1.

Row 2 P1 *k2, p6, k2, p12 rep from * to
last 11 sts, k2, p6, k2, p1.

Rep rows 1 & 2 twice more.

Row 7 K1 *p2, C6B, p2, k12 rep from *
to last 11 sts, p2, C6B, p2, k1.

Row 8 As row 2.

Rows 9 and 10 As rows 1 and 2.

Row 11 *K12, p2, k6, p2 rep from * to
last 12 sts, k12.

Row 12 *P12, k2, p6, k2 rep from * to
last 12 sts, p12.

Rep rows 11 & 12 twice more.

Row 17 *K12, p2, C6B, p2 rep from *
to last 12 sts, k12.

Row 18 As row 12.

Rows 19 and 20 As rows 11 and 12.

These 20 rows form the cable patt.
Rep until back measures 13[15]in
(33[38]cm), ending on a WS row.

Shape shoulders

K22[27] sts. Turn. Work on these sts only.

Next row P2tog, purl to end 21[26]sts.

Next row Cast off.

Slip centre 20[24] sts onto holder.
With RS facing, rejoin yarn to second
side, knit to end.

Next row Purl to last 2 sts, p2 to 21[26] sts.
Cast off.

FRONT

Work as for back until work measures
12 rows less, ending on a WS row.

Shape neck

Patt 25[31] sts. Leave rem sts on spare
needle.

Work on these sts only.

Dec 1 st at neck edge on every alt row
until 21[26] sts rem.

Keeping to patt, work even until front
measures the same as back, ending
on a WS row.

Cast off.

Slip centre 14[16] sts onto holder.

With RS facing, rejoin yarn to second
side and work to match the first,
reversing all shapings.

Cable chart 1   64[78] sts x 20 rows

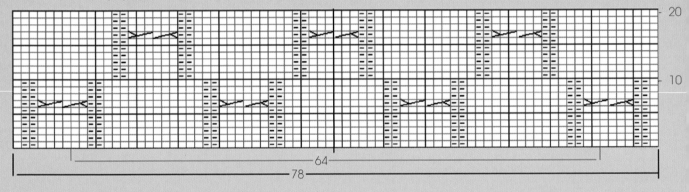

Cable chart 2   64[78] sts x 20 rows

KEY

Knit on RS, purl on WS

− Purl on RS, knit on WS

C6B

Each square = 1 st and 1 row
Read RS rows (knit) from R to L and WS
rows (purl) from L to R.

SLEEVES

Using 4.5mm (US7) needles, cast on 34 sts.

Beg with a knit row, st st 4 rows.

Work double rib as before for 4 rows, inc 1st at each end of last row (36 sts).

Change to 5mm (US8) needles.

Beg 20 row cable patt as set for 2nd size at same time inc 1 st at each end of row on 1st and every alt row, 3 times (42 sts) and then on every 4th row until 56[66] sts. Treat all increases as stocking stitches.

Work even until sleeve measures 9[10] in (23[25.5]cm), ending on a WS row. Cast off.

NECK

Darn in loose yarn ends and sew right shoulder seam.

Using 4.5mm (US7) needles, PUK 8[10] sts down front left neck, 14[16] sts from centre holder, 8[10] sts up right front neck, 2 sts down back shoulder, 20[24] sts across back holder, 2 sts up left shoulder 56[64] sts.

Double rib for 5 rows.

Beg with a knit row, st st 4 rows.

Cast off loosely.

MAKING UP

Darn in all loose yarn ends. Sew neck and left shoulder seam. Pin, then sew sleeves to armhole edge. Sew side seams.

hemp swing dress & trousers

This fasionable dress and trouser combination is knitted in mouthwatering lime and pink with pretty daisy buttons to finish the dress perfectly. In cool and breathable hemp, this outfit is great for summer picnics or sandcastles on the beach.

Sizes

	6–12 months	1–2 years	2–3 years
TROUSERS			
Finished waist	22in	24in	26in
	56cm	61cm	66cm
Total length	16½in	18in	20in
	42cm	46cm	51cm
DRESS			
Actual chest	22in	24in	26in
	56cm	61cm	66cm
Length from shoulder	13in	15in	16in
	33cm	38cm	41cm

Materials

TROUSERS

House of Hemp 4-ply
(85m/93yd per 50g skein)
1[1:2] x 50g skein in Om
2[2:3] x 50g skein in Yippi
Elastic for waist

DRESS

4[4:6] x 50g skein in Om
5 x daisy buttons (by Stockwell Pottery,
see *Suppliers*, page 142)
3.5 (US4) needles
4mm (US6) needles
Stitch holder

Tension

20 sts x 30 rows over 4in (10cm)

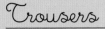

Trousers

FRONT AND BACK

(make 2 pieces alike)
Using 3.5mm (US4) needles and Yippi,
cast on 56[60:66] sts.

Work casing

Beg with a knit row, work 5 rows st st.

Next row (Turning row) Knit.
Change to 4mm (US6) needles and
beg with a knit row, work in st st for
a further 7[7½:8]in (18[19:20.5]cm),
ending on a purl row. At the same time
work stripe sequence as follows:
4 rows Yippi
2 rows Om

Divide for first leg

Keeping to stripe sequence, work as
follows:
Next row K25[27:30], turn. Work on
these sts only. Leave rem 31[33:36]sts
on holder.
Work even in stripe patt until leg
measures 9[10:11½]in (23[25.5:29]cm),
ending on a knit row.
Garter stitch 3 rows.
Cast off.

Second leg

With RS facing and keeping to stripe
patt, rejoin yarn to rem stitches.
Next row Cast off 6 sts, knit to end
25[27:30] sts.
Complete second leg to match
the first.

MAKING UP

Darn in loose yarn ends and press
pieces. Join front and back gusset
seams. Join side and inside leg seams.
Fold down waistband casing to WS of
trousers and slip stitch in place leaving
a small opening for threading elastic.
Thread elastic onto a safety pin and
thread through waistband. Adjust to
correct waist size and stitch elastic
ends securely together. Sew
up opening.

knitknack

Don't be afraid to handle hemp.
The more it is worn, washed,
ironed and loved, the softer and
lovelier hemp becomes.

Dress

BACK

*Using 3.5mm (US4) needles and Om, cast on 70[76:80] sts.

Garter stitch 4 rows.

Change to 4mm (US6) needles.

Row 1 K2, sl1, k1, psso, knit to last 4 sts, k2tog, k2, 68[74:78] sts.

Beg with a purl row, work in st st for 5 rows.

Rep these 6 rows until 56[60:66] sts.

Work even until skirt measures 7[8½:9]in (18[22:23]cm), ending with a knit row.

Next row Knit. **

Work even in st st for a further 2in (5cm), ending on a purl row.

Shape armholes

Cast off 3 sts at beg of next 2 rows, 50[54:60] sts.

Dec 1 st at each end of next and foll alt rows until 40[44:48] sts.

Work even until work measures 11½(13½,14½)in 29(34.5:37)cm, ending on a purl row.

Shape shoulders

Next row K11[12:12], turn. Work on these sts only.

Dec 1 st on neck edge on next and foll alt rows until 8 sts.

Work even until armhole measures 4[4½:5]in (10[11.5:13]cm), ending on a purl row.

Cast off.

Slip centre 18[20:24] sts onto stitch holder.

Rejoin yarn to second side. Rep as for first side, rev shapings to match.

LEFT FRONT

Work as for back from * to **.

Shape left slope

Next row Knit.

Next row Cast off 3 sts at beg of row, purl to end 53[57:63] sts.

Rep last 2 rows, twice more 47[51:57] sts.

Dec 1 st at neck edge on every row until 37[41:47] sts.

Shape armhole

Cast off 3 sts at beg of next row, knit to last 2 sts, k2tog 33[37:43] sts.

Next row P2tog, purl to end 32[36:42] sts.

Next row K2tog, knit to last to 2 sts, k2tog 30[34:40] sts.

Rep last 2 rows until 18[22:28] sts rem.

Dec 1 st on neck edge only until 8 sts.

Work even until front measures 13[15:16]in (33[38:41]cm), ending on a purl row.

Cast off.

RIGHT FRONT

Work as for left front, reversing all shapings.

MAKING UP

Darn all loose yarn ends and press
pieces. Sew both shoulder seams.

Armhole bands

With RS facing and using 3.5mm
(US4) needles, PUK 38[44:48] sts along
armhole edge.
Garter stitch 3 rows.
Cast off loosely.
Rep for second armhole.
Sew side seams.

Neck band

With RS facing and using 3.5mm (US4)
needles, PUK 50[56:58] sts up right
front slope, 6 sts down back shoulder,
18[20:24] sts from centre back holder,
6 sts up rear left shoulder, 50[56:58] sts
down left front slope, 130[144:152] sts
Garter stitch 3 rows.
Cast off loosely.
Press into shape and wrap right
front across left front. Position the
daisy buttons just above the garter
stitch waist and sew in place through
both layers.

wool tank top & hat

This chunky hat can be worn two ways; either buttoned up like a classic deerstalker or with earflaps down on snowy days. However your toddler likes to wear it, they'll look smart with the matching wide-rib tank top.

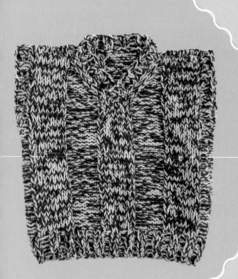

Sizes

	1–2 years	2–3 years
Finished waist	12in	14in
	30.5cm	36cm
Length from shoulder	13in	14in
	33cm	36cm
Head circumference	16in	18in
	41cm	46cm

Materials

Cornish Organic Wool DK
(231m/251yd per 100g skein)
2 x 100g skeins in Natural
2 x 100g skeins in St Just
7mm (US10.5) straight and circular
needles.
3 x stitch holders
3 x buttons (by Stockwell Pottery, see
Suppliers, page 142)

Tension

14 sts x 20 rows over 4in (10cm)

Tank top

FRONT

*Using 7mm (US10.5) needles and
one strand of natural and St Just held
together, cast on 40[48] sts.
Work rib as follows:
Row 1 (K2, p2) rep to end.
Repeat this row 7 more times (8 rows
in total).
1st size
Row 1 (RS) (K8, p8) rep once more, k8.
Row 2 (WS) (P8, k8) rep once more, p8.
2nd size
Row 1 (RS) P4(k8, p8) rep to last 4 sts, p4.
Row 2 (WS) K4(p8, k8) rep to last 4 sts, k4.
Rep these 2 patt rows until work
measures 8[9]in (20.5[23]cm), ending on
a WS row.

Shape armholes

Keeping to patt, cast off 3 sts at beg of
next 2 rows. 34[42] sts. **

Divide for neck

1st size K5, p8, k4, turn (17 sts). Leave
rem sts on holder.

Row 2 P4, k8, p5.

2nd size P1, k8, p8, k4, turn (21 sts).
Leave rem sts on holder.

Row 2 P4, k8, p8, k1.

Decrease as follows – all sizes

Next row Patt to last 4 sts, k2tog, k2.

Next row Patt to end.

Cont decreasing as set until 8[12] sts.
Work even in patt until armhole
measures 5in (13cm), ending on
a WS row.
Cast off.

BACK

Work as for front from * to **.
Work even in patt until armhole
measures 5in (13cm), ending on
a WS row.

Shape shoulders

Row 1 Patt 9[13] sts. Turn.

Row 2 K2tog, patt to end 8[12] sts.
Cast off.
Slip centre 16 sts onto holder.
Rejoin yarn to second side.

Row 1 Patt to end.

Row 2 Patt to last 2 sts, k2tog 8[12] sts.
Cast off.

MAKING UP

Pin and block pieces. Darn in loose
yarn ends. Sew shoulder seams.

Sleeve band

With RS facing and using 7mm (US10.5)
needles and one strand of natural and
St Just held together, PUK 44 sts along
first sleeve edge.
K2, p2 rib for 3 rows.
Cast off loosely.
Rep for second side.

Neckband

With RS facing and using circular
needle, start at the point of the front
'V' and PUK 18 sts up front right neck
edge, 16 sts from back holder and 18
sts down left front neck edge (52 sts).
Use the circular needle like straight
needles and work back and forth.
Work 3 rows in k2, p2 rib.
Cast off loosely.
Sew side seams of tank. Overlap
centre front bands of 'V' and slip stitch
neatly in place.

Hat

EARFLAPS

(make 2)

Using 7mm (US10.5) needles and one strand of natural and St Just held together, cast on 6 sts.

St st 2 rows.

Buttonhole row Kfb, k1,cast off 2 sts, k1, kfb.

Next row P3, cast on 2 sts, p3 (8 sts).

Next row Kfb, knit to last st, kfb (10 sts).

Next row Purl.

Rep last 2 rows until 14 sts.

Work even until earflap measure 3in (8cm), ending on a purl row.

Leave stitches on holder

FRONT FLAP

(make 1)

Using 7mm (US10.5) needles and one strand of natural and St Just held together, cast on 8 sts.

St st 2 rows.

Buttonhole row Kfb, k2, cast off 2 sts, k2, kfb.

Next row P4, cast on 2 sts, p4 (10 sts).

Next row Kfb, knit to last st, kfb (12 sts).

Next row Purl.

Rep last 2 rows until 14[18]sts.

Work 4[0] more rows in st st, ending on a purl row.

Leave sts on holder.

MAIN HAT

Using 7mm (US10.5) needles and one strand of natural and St Just held together, cast on 7[9] sts, knit across 14 sts from first earflap, knit across 14[18] sts from front flap, knit across 14 sts from second earflap, cast on 7[9] sts (56[64] sts).

Next row Knit.

1st size

Row 1 (RS) P8(k8, p8) rep to last 8 sts, p8.

Row 2 (WS) K8 [p8, k8] rep to last 8 sts, k8.

2nd size

Row 1 (RS) K4(p8, k8) rep to last 4 sts, k4.

Row 2 (WS) P4 (k8, p8) rep to last 4 sts, p4.

Rep these 2 patt rows until hat measures 5[6]in (13[15.5]cm), ending on a WS row.

Dec for crown

Row 1 (K2, k2tog) rep to end, 42[48] sts.

Row 2 Patt.

Row 3 (K1, k2tog) rep to end, 28[32] sts.

Row 4 Patt.

Row 5 (K2tog) rep to end, 14[16] sts.

Row 6 As row 5, 7[8] sts.

Break yarn, thread through st and pull tight.

Press hat lightly, darn in loose yarn ends and sew rear seam. Position buttons and sew firmly in place.

PART THREE

Accessories

changing bag & bottle tote

This handy changing bag also doubles up as a changing mat. It is ideal for storing all the essential equipment and has a useful front pocket too. The drawstring bottle tote stores away baby's milk and keeps it warm until you need it.

Size

16 x 26in (41 x 66cm)

Materials

Cornish Organic DK Wool (230m/251yd per 100g ball)
2 x 100g balls of St Mawes (Navy)
1 x 100g ball each of shades St Eval (Green), St Hilary (Amber), St Blazey (Pink), St Ives (Royal Blue)
4mm (US6) needles
3mm (US3) needles
2 stitch holders
10 Frog Prince buttons (by Injabulo, see *Suppliers* page 142)
17.5 x 27in (44 x 69cm) organic calico

Tension

20 sts x 28 rows over 4in (10cm)

Changing bag

STRAPS (make 2)
Using 4mm (US6) needles, cast on 12 sts in St Mawes.
Moss st 6 rows as follows:
Row 1 *(K1, p1) rep from * to end.
Row 2 *(P1, k1) rep from * to end.
Rep these 2 rows, 3 times.
Beg stripe sequence as follows:
2 rows of garter stitch each in St Eval, St Hilary, St Blazey, St Ives and St Mawes.
Rep this stripe sequence until strap measures 28in (71cm).
Change to St Mawes and moss st 6 rows as before.
Cast off.

MAKING UP

Trim all loose ends and fold the strap in half lengthwise with RS facing. Tuck all loose ends into the centre of the strap and join the long seam using ladder stitch.

RAINBOW POCKET

Using 4mm (US6) needles
and St Mawes, cast on 40 sts.
Working in st st, work the stripe
sequence as before until pocket
measures 7in (18cm), ending on
a WS row.
Leave stitches on a holder.

BODY OF THE BAG

Using 4mm (US6) needles and
St Mawes, cast on 80 sts.
Work 6 rows in moss st as for straps.
Next row Moss 6, knit to last 6 sts, moss 6.
Next row Moss 6, purl to last 6 sts, moss 6.
Rep the last 2 rows until bag measures
13in (33cm), ending on a WS row.
This is the halfway point of the bag.
Place coloured yarn markers here
for reference.
Before you move on, mark the position
of the buttons (5 on each vertical
moss stitch band, *see photo for
reference*) on the WS of the bag.
Cont working in patt as before, but
keep folding the bag at its halfway
point to locate the button markers.
Insert buttonholes at corresponding
points on RS rows as follows:
Buttonhole rows Moss 2, yf, p2tog,
moss 2, knit to last 6 sts, moss 2, yf,
p2tog, moss 2.
Cont in this way until bag measures
22in (56cm), ending on WS row.

PLACE POCKET

Moss 6, k14, place next 40 sts on
holder, with RS of pocket facing,
knit the 40 sts from holder, k14,
moss 6. Cont as before, working the
buttonholes until all 10 are complete
(5 holes on each side) and work
measures 25in (63.5cm), ending
on a WS row.
Moss st 6 rows.
Cast off.

MAKING UP

With St Mawes and 4mm (US6)
needles, cast off the 40 sts of front
pocket. Darn in all loose yarn ends
and pin and block the bag so it is
square. Make a flag edging long
enough to fit the pocket top *(see box
on page 114)*. Sew edging in place
with small neat stitches. Sew the sides
and bottom of the rainbow pocket to
the WS side of the bag. Sew buttons
firmly in place. Open the bag flat
and pin straps in position. Sew firmly in
place along the bottom of the moss
stitch edging of the bag. Make a
calico lining by folding ½in (1.5cm) of
fabric onto WS around edges. Place
on WS of mat, covering strap ends.
Slip stitch around all edges.

knitknack

Make calico pockets and sew them
in place on the bag's lining for
extra storage space.

flag edging

Flag edging is a useful and easy trim for a whole host of projects. It has been used here to add interest to the tote opening, but it is just as pretty stitched onto lower edges of sweaters, cardigans or on sock tops for a quirky cuff trim. For edging the bottle tote, follow the instructions below and then sew firmly along top edge.

Using 3mm (US3) needles, cast on 2 sts.
Row 1 Inc 1, k1 (3 sts).
Row 2 K1, p1, inc 1 (4 sts).
Row 3 Inc 1, k1, p1, k1 (5 sts).
Row 4 (K1, p1) twice, inc 1 (6 sts).
Row 5 Moss stitch without increasing.
Rows 6–9 Cont in moss st, dec at shaped edge on every row until 2 sts.
Row 10 K2.
Rep these 10 rows until edging is at required length.
Cast off.

Bottle tote

Using 4mm (US6) needles and St Mawes, cast on 40 sts.
Beg with a knit row, st st 4 rows.
Eyelet row K3, yf, k2tog (k4, yf, k2tog) rep to last 3 sts, k3.
Work in st st until work measures 10in (25cm), ending on WS row.
Cast off.

MAKING UP

Pin and block work so it is square.
Optional Swiss darn coloured spots (instructions on page 138) randomly over work *(see box, right)*. Make a flag edging *(see box, left)* in St Mawes as before and sew firmly in place along top edge.

Fold tote in half lengthwise with RS facing and sew bottom and side seam. Turn RS out. Make a 22in (56cm) tie by plaiting 6 strands of St Mawes and knotting each end. Thread through eyelet holes and pull tight.

colour spots

Use the chart below to add coloured spots randomly over the bottle tote. Swiss darn the spots, following the instructions on page 138.

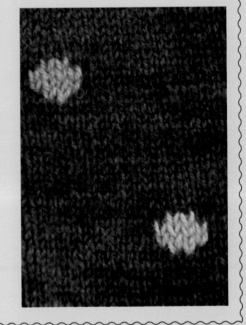

Colour spot chart

corn fibre burp cloth & bib

This pretty cloth and matching bib is designed to mop up those inevitable milky spills. It fits perfectly across your shoulder, so you can rub baby's back in comfort, without fear of staining your favourite shirt.

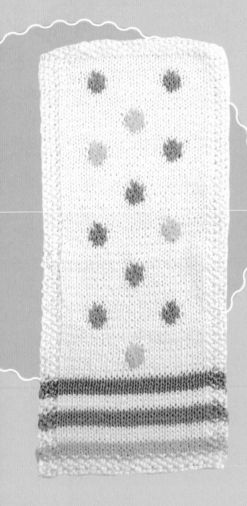

Sizes

Burp cloth 15 x 7in (38 x 18cm)
Bib 6in wide x 6.5in long at centre (15 x 16cm)

Materials

SWTC Amaizing 100% Corn fibre (130m/142yd per 50g ball)
BURP CLOTH
1 x 50g ball each in shades Cream Puff, Ducky, Princess and Keepsake.
BIB
1 x 50g ball each in shades Cream Puff, Ducky, Princess and Keepsake
4.5mm (US7) needles

Tension

24 sts x 32 rows over 4in (10cm)

Burp cloth

Using 4.5mm (US7) needles and Cream Puff, cast on 36sts.
Row 1 *(K1, p1) rep from * to end.
Row 2 *(P1, k1) rep from * to end.
Rep these 2 moss st rows once more.
Beg chart patt and work to end.
Rep rows 1–22 of the chart once more.
Change to Princess and beg stripe patt.
Keeping moss st edging, work stripe patt in st st (beg with a knit row) as follows:
4 rows in Princess.
4 rows in Cream Puff.
4 rows in Keepsake.
4 rows in Cream Puff.
4 rows in Ducky.
Finally, work rows 1 and 2 twice (4 rows in total).
Cast off.
Darn in loose yarn ends.

Burp cloth chart   36 sts x 59 rows

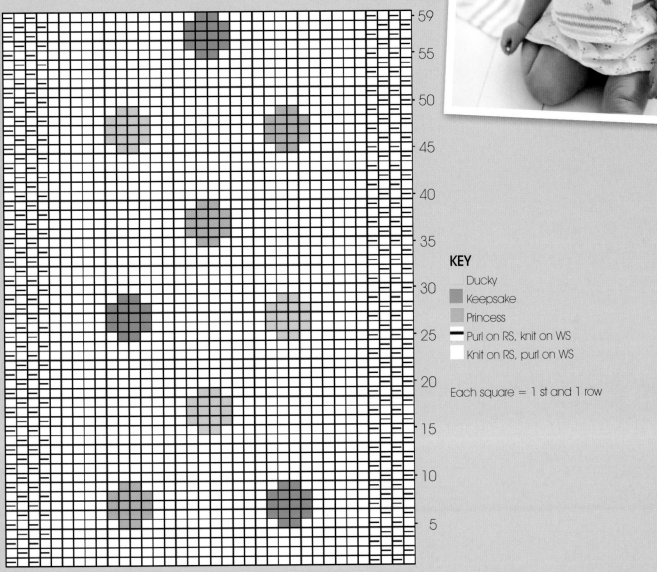

59
55
50
45
40
35
30
25
20
15
10
5

KEY

Ducky
Keepsake
Princess
Purl on RS, knit on WS
Knit on RS, purl on WS

Each square = 1 st and 1 row

Bib

Using 4.5mm (US7) needles and
Cream Puff, cast on 24 sts.
Work in moss st as follows:
Row 1 *(K1,p1) rep from * to end.
Row 2 *(P1, k1) rep from * to end.
Change to Ducky. Work increases as
folls:
Row 3 K1, p1, inc 1 in next st, k18,
inc 1 in next st k1, p1 (26 sts).
Row 4 P1, k1, p22, p1, k1.
Change to Cream Puff.
Row 5 K1, p1, inc 1 in next st, k20,
inc 1 in next st, k1, p1 (28 sts).
Row 6 P1, k1, p26, p1, k1.
Change to Keepsake.
Row 7 K1, p1 inc 1 in next st, k22,
inc 1 in next st, k1, p1 (30 sts).
Row 8 P1, k1, p26, p1, k1.
Change to Cream Puff.
Row 9 K1, p1, inc 1 in next st, k24,
inc 1 in next st, k1, p1 (32 sts).
Row 10 P1, k1, p28, p1, k1.
Change to Princess.
Row 11 K1, p1, inc 1 in next st k26,
inc 1 in next st k1, p1 (34 sts).
Row 12 P1, k1, p30, p1, k1.
Change to Cream Puff.
Row 13 K1, p1, inc 1 in next st, k28,
inc 1 in next st, k1, p1 (36 sts).
Row 14 P1, k1, p32, p1, k1.
Beg working from row 1 of chart and
foll until complete.

SHAPE NECK

Next row K1, p1, k10, leave rem st on
holder. Turn and work on these 12 st
as follows:
Next row P10, p1, k1.
Next row K1, p1, k2tog, k6, k2tog
(10 sts).
Next row P8, p1, k1.
Next row K1, p1, k2tog, k4, k2tog (8 sts).
Next row P6, p1, k1.
Rep decreases as set until 4 sts rem.
Next row K2tog, twice (2 sts).

TIES

Work in st st on these 2 sts until tie
measures 7in (18cm), ending on
a purl row.
Cast off.

Put centre 12sts on a stitch holder.
Rejoin yarn to second side and rep
as for first side, reversing all shapings.

NECKBAND

Using Cream Puff, 4.5mm (US7)
needles and with RS facing, pick
up and knit 9 sts down left side of
neck, knit across the 12 sts from
holder, pick up and knit 9 sts up
right side of neck (30 sts).
Moss st 2 rows.
Cast off.

Bib chart   36 sts x 33 rows

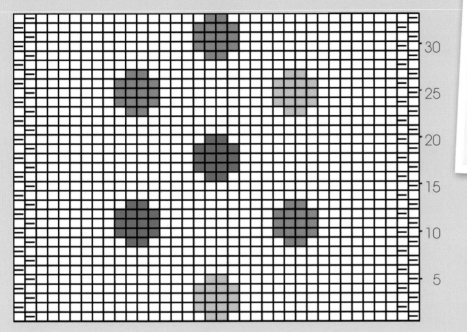

KEY

Ducky
Keepsake
Princess
Purl on RS, knit on WS
Knit on RS, purl on WS

Each square = 1 st and 1 row

soy silk nappy liner

This 100% soy silk nappy liner is wonderfully soft and absorbent, providing an extra layer that can double the life of your cloth nappies. Three sizes are shown, so you can use them right the way through from birth to potty training.

Sizes

	small	medium	large
Finished length	11½in	13in	15in
	29cm	33cm	38cm
Finished width	4in	4½in	5in
	10cm	11.5cm	13cm

Materials

SWTC Infinity 100% Soy silk
(100m/109yd per 50g ball)
4.5mm (US7) needles
Small amount of contrast thread for
blanket stitch edging
Large-eyed needle

Tension

24sts x 28 rows to 4in (10cm)

Nappy liner (make 2)

Using Infinity and 4.5mm (US7) needles,
cast on 24[28:30] sts.
Working in st st and beg with a knit row,
inc 1 st at each end of next and every
foll alt row until 30[34:36] sts.
Work in st st for 17 rows.
Dec by k2tog at each end of next and
every foll alt row until 22[28:30] sts.
Work even in st st until liner measures
8½[10:12]in (22[25.5:30.5]cm), ending
on a purl row.
Inc 1 st at each end of next and every
foll alt row until 30[34:36] sts.
Work in st st for 17 rows.
Dec by k2tog at each end of next
and every foll alt row until 24[28:30] sts,
ending on a purl row.
Cast off.

blanket stitch

Working from left to right. The twisted edge should lie on the outer edge of fabric to form a raised line. Bring needle up at point **A**, down at **B** and up at **C** with thread looped under the needle. Pull through. Take care to tighten the stitches equally. Repeat to the right. Fasten the last loop by taking a small stitch along the lower line.

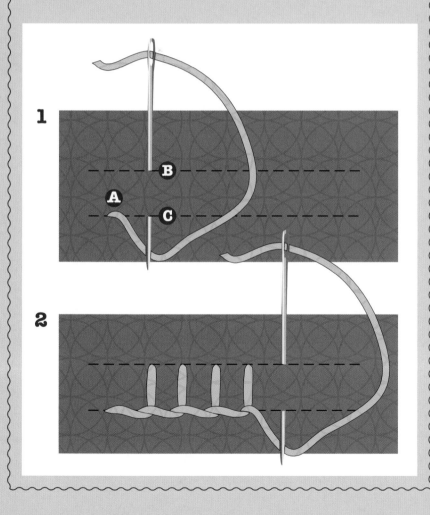

MAKING UP

Darn loose yarns ends and press both pieces lightly. Place RS tog and sew around edge leaving a small opening for turning. Turn RS out and close opening with small, neat stitches. Take contrast thread and work a row of blanket stitch around the edge of liner. Fasten off.

soy silk

Soy silk yarn is produced sustainably from soy protein that is a by-product of tofu manufacturing. Used here undyed, it is natural, soft, warm and has excellent wicking properties.

bamboo nursing pads

These nursing pads are knitted in 100% bamboo, which is renowned for its wicking properties – making it the perfect choice for this project. Pick different coloured yarns to match your bras, then simply use, wash and use again.

Sizes

4in (10cm) diameter

Materials

SWTC Bamboo
(228m/250yd per 100g ball)
1 x 100g ball of black (shade 126) or white (shade 146)
3mm (US3) needles
2.5mm (USC/2) crochet hook

Tension

28 sts x 32 rows to 4in (10cm)

Nursing pad

(make 2)
Using 3mm (US3) needles and cast on 6 sts.
Working in garter st throughout, inc 1 st at each end of next and foll alt row until 22 sts.
Work 17 rows of garter st.
Dec by k2tog at each end of next and every foll alt row until 6 sts rem.
Cast off.

EDGING

Using a 2.5mm (USC/2) crochet hook, rejoin yarn to any edge with a sl st.
Next row 1ch, work a round of dc evenly around the nursing pad, ending with a sl st into the first ch of round.
See page 139 for double crochet instructions.
Fasten off.
Darn in loose yarn ends.

knitknack

If you are new to crochet, this is
an ideal project to try out double
crochet. The beauty of crochet is
that if you are not happy with it,
you can just pull it out and start
again without having to worry
about dropped stitches
and tiresome ladders.

alpaca lavender pillow

When baby is in bed, relax with this soft, alpaca rest pillow. It hugs the neck and has an opening for a microwavable wheat bag to soothe away aches and pains. Add a few drops of lavender oil for an extra special pampering experience.

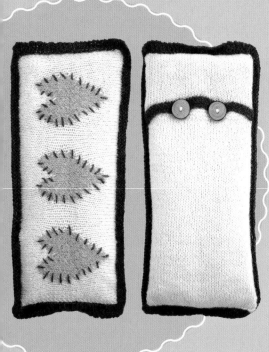

Size

14 x 7in (36 x 17cm) including edging

Materials

Artesano Alpaca (100%) Inca Cloud (120m/131yd per 50g ball)
1 x 50g ball each in shades Oatmeal, Chocolate and Cream
3.5mm (US4) needles
2 x wooden buttons
1 x wheat bag 12 x 6in (30.5 x 15cm)
Lavender essential oil

Tension

25 sts x 33 rows to 4in (10cm)

Pillow

FRONT

Using 3.5mm (US4) needles and Chocolate, cast on 83 sts.
Garter st 4 rows.
Row 5 K4 in Chocolate, k75 in Cream, k4 in Chocolate.

Row 6 K4 in Chocolate, p75 in Cream, k4 in Chocolate.
Rep rows 5 and 6, 5 times
(10 rows in total).
Next row K4 in Chocolate, beg working chart patt opposite, K4 in Chocolate.
Cont to work the chart until complete, working 4 knit sts in Chocolate at each end of the row as set.
Next row As row 6.
Next row Rep rows 5 and 6, 5 times
(10 rows in total).
Garter st 4 rows in Chocolate.
Cast off.

BACK FLAPS

Lower (make 1)
Using 3.5mm (US4) needles and Cream, cast on 38 sts.
Garter st 2 rows.
Beg with a knit row, work even in st st for 9½in (23cm) ending on a purl row.
Cast off.
Upper (make 1)
Using 3.5mm (US4) needles and Chocolate cast on 38 sts.

Garter st 2 rows.

Buttonhole row K12, yf, k2tog, k11, yf, k2tog, k12.

Garter st 1 more row.

Change to Cream.

Beg with a knit row, work even in st st until work measures 3in (8cm).

Cast off.

MAKING UP

Darn in loose yarn ends and press lightly. Using Chocolate, copy the patchwork embroidery around each heart *(see photo)* using single, long stitches. With WS tog, place the back flaps in place and pin. Using small neat stitches, sew in place. Position the wood buttons and sew firmly. Dot the wheat cushion with lavender oil and insert into the pillow.

Heart chart   75 sts x 29 rows

KEY

■ Chocolate
□ Oatmeal

Each square = 1 st and 1 row
Read RS rows (knit) from R to L and WS rows (purl) from L to R.

knitknack

You can make your own wheat cushion using two pieces of calico 13 x 7in (33 x 18cm). This includes a ½in (1cm) seam allowance. Stitch around three sides, turn right side out and fill with wheat. Stitch up the fourth side and the cushion is complete.

PART FOUR

Knitting basics

getting started

Buying yarn

It is a good idea to buy the yarns specified in the patterns so that you will be sure the finished garment will look every bit as good as the picture. Details of suppliers are included at the back of the book. Do try contacting them online if you are not sure where to purchase a specific yarn type. Their sales department will be able to put you in contact with your local stockist or online supplier so you should find it a relatively straightforward process to match everything up.

Sizing

The sizes for each garment are given at the beginning of every pattern. I have tried to include a wide range of sizes appropriate to each project. However, all babies vary in size so don't be afraid to alter sleeve and sweater lengths if necessary.

DYE LOTS

Remember, yarn is always dyed in batches or lots so when purchasing, always check the dye lot on the ball band carefully. Make sure all the numbers match otherwise your finished garment might turn out to be a disappointment if there is colour variation when you change balls. This is even more important when selecting yarn dyed using organic colours where the finished product can vary quite significantly from batch to batch. Make sure you order plenty of the same dye lot and ask for a 'lay-by' service if you're not sure of your amounts.

YARN SUBSTITUTION

If you choose to substitute the yarns recommended on the pattern there are several pointers to bear in mind. Firstly, always choose the same weight yarn to substitute with ie: Double Knit, chunky, Aran etc.

Secondly, check the yardage on your preferred yarn, which will be written on the ball band. There may be less or more per ball than on the recommended type. In this case, you will need to allow for extra or less balls, so take time to work it out carefully.

Finally, always knit up a tension swatch in your substitute yarn before beginning the project. You need to do this to check the stitch sizes match and the finished garment will come out the correct size. Also, it will give you a better idea of how the whole thing is going to look.

Tension swatches

To knit a tension swatch, cast on 40 stitches using the recommended needle size. Work in pattern for 4in (10cm) minimum before casting off loosely. Next, lay the swatch out on a flat surface and place a flat ruler vertically on top. Count the number of rows over 4in (10cm). Then do the same horizontally but this time count the number of stitches over 4in (10cm).

If you have more stitches and rows per 4in (10cm) than stated on the pattern, try knitting the whole thing again using larger needles. Likewise if you have fewer stitches and rows per 4in (10cm), repeat with smaller needles. Keep working at it until your tension matches that of the pattern.

Following patterns

Before you begin knitting, always read the pattern through from beginning to end. It's a good idea to underline or highlight the size you are knitting throughout the pattern. That way, you know exactly where you are at a glance. Figures for larger sizes are given in square brackets and where only one figure appears, this applies to all sizes. Next, check any abbreviations you are not sure of against the list on page 141 and just like following a recipe, gather all your yarn and tools together before you start.

Reading charts

Some of the patterns use cable and colour charts. As in all knitting charts, one square represents one stitch and one line of squares is equal to one row.

On right side rows, read the chart from right to left and on wrong side rows, do the opposite ie: read from left to right. Begin knitting from the bottom right side corner of the chart at Row 1. Carry on to Row 2 and 3 and so on until the chart is complete.

You will see that every square has either a symbol or colour marked on it. Read the accompanying key to understand which colour or stitch you need to use to complete the row.

A chart ruler (available from most good haberdashers or yarn stores) is an excellent investment. You can clip it onto the chart and move it up or down the rows once you've completed it. That way you won't get muddled or lost in the middle.

Some charts like fair isle or cable have 'repeats' included in them. In this case, complete the whole chart to the end and then start again at Row 1.

basic techniques

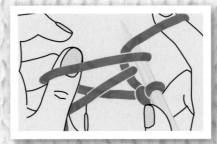

CASTING ON

1 Make a slip knot a fair distance from the end of the yarn and place onto needle. Pull knot tight to make first stitch.

2 Hold needle in right hand and wrap loose tail end around your left thumb from front to back. Push point of needle through the thumb loop from front to back. Wind the ball end of yarn around the needle from left to right.

3 Pull loop through thumb loop and remove thumb. Gently pull the new loop tight using the tail yarn. Repeat until you have desired amount of stitches on needle.

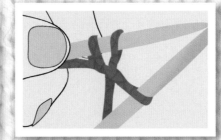
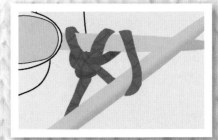

CABLE CAST ON

1 Hold needle with the slip knot in your left hand. Put tip of right-hand needle through the stitch from front to back. Wrap yarn round right-hand needle tip in an anti-clockwise direction.

2 Bring the right hand-needle with the yarn wrapped around it, back through the stitch towards you.

3 Slip the loop of yarn you have just made back onto the tip of the left

needle and pull gently on the ball end of yarn to tighten stitch slightly. You should now have two stitches on your left needle. To make more stitches, follow steps 1–3 until you have required amount on left-hand needle.

KNIT STITCH

1 Hold needle with stitches in left hand. Hold yarn at back of work and insert point of right-hand empty needle into the front loop of the first stitch. Wrap yarn around point of right-hand needle in a clockwise direction using your index finger. Bring yarn through to front of work.

2 With yarn still wrapped around the point, bring the right-hand needle back towards you through the loop of the first stitch. Try to keep the free yarn fairly taut but not too slack or tight.

3 Finally, with the new stitch firmly on the right hand-needle, gently pull the old stitch to the right and off the tip of the left-hand needle. Repeat for all the knit stitches across the row.

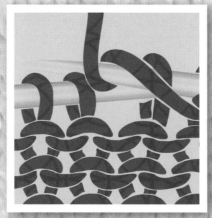
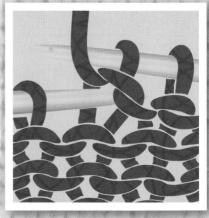

PURL STITCH

1 Hold needles with stitches in left hand. Hold yarn at front of work and insert point of right-hand empty needle into the front loop of the first stitch.

2 Wrap yarn around point of right-hand needle in and anti-clockwise direction using index finger. Bring yarn back to front of work.

3 Now, with yarn still wrapped around point of right-hand needle, bring it back through the stitch. Try to keep free yarn taut but not too slack or tight. Finally, with the new stitch firmly on the right-hand needle, gently pull the old stitch off the tip of the left-hand needle. Repeat for all the purl stitches along the row.

GARTER STITCH

Knit every row.

STOCKING STITCH

Knit on right-side rows and purl on wrong-side rows.

MOSS STITCH

Worked over an even number of stitches:

Row 1 (K1,p1) to end.
Row 2 (P1,k1) to end.
Rep rows 1 and 2 to form patt.

Worked over an odd number of stitches:

Row 1 *K1,p1, rep fom * to last st, k1.
Rep row 1 to form patt.

SINGLE RIB

Worked over even number of stitches:
Row 1 (K1,p1) to end.
Rep row 1 to form patt.

Worked over odd number of stitches:
Row 1 (K1,p1) rep to last st, k1.
Row 2 (P1,k1) rep to last st, k1.
Rep rows 1 and 2 to form patt.

DOUBLE RIB

Row 1 (K2,p2) rep to end.
Rep row 1 to form patt.

CASTING OFF

1 Knit first 2 stitches. Push point of left needle through the first stitch and lift over the second stitch. One stitch remains on the right needle.

2 Knit another stitch from left needle and repeat steps 1 and 2. Repeat until you have one stitch left. Cut yarn leaving a long tail and thread it through remaining stitch and pull tight.

SEWING UP (MATTRESS STITCH)

For invisible seams always sew pieces together using matching yarn. Place pieces to be joined side by side on a flat surface with right side facing towards you. Take a threaded needle and secure to fabric by weaving down the side edge of one of the pieces. Bring the needle out between the first and second stitches. Working vertically, bring the needle back up through the opposite piece and insert into first row again from front to back bringing it up below the horizontal strand. Go back to first piece and keep stitching in this way. You will see your stitches form a ladder along the seam. Pull tight every few stitches to close fabric neatly.

COLOUR KNITTING (INTARSIA)

This technique is used when knitting blocks of colour. Use separate bobbins of yarn for each isolated area of colour. Using whole balls can result in messy tangles. Bobbins are smaller and hang at the back of the work out of the way. When you need to change colours mid-row, make sure you twist the old and new yarns together at the back of your work to join the blocks of colour properly and to avoid holes. Don't worry if your work doesn't look perfect. When you have finished the piece, weave in the ends carefully at the back with a tapestry needle and press lightly under a damp cloth (unless the ball band on the yarn states not to iron), easing any distorted stitches back into line. This makes all the difference and can transform the neatness of your colour knitting.

CABLES

Cables are formed by crossing one set of stitches over another. To do this you need a cable needle to hold stitches at either the back or front of the work whilst the same number of stitches are worked from the left needle.

Cable 4 sts front (4 sts cbfr)

1 Slip the first 2 stitches onto the cable needle and hold to the front of work.

2 Knit the next 2 stitches on the left-hand needle. Slip the 2 stitches from the cable needle back onto the left-hand needle and knit as usual.

Cable 4 sts back (4 sts cbbk) *(above)*

Slip the first 2 stitches onto the cable needle and hold to back of work. Knit the next 2 stitches on the left-hand needle. Slip the 2 stitches from the cable needle back onto the left-hand needle and knit as usual.

CIRCULAR KNITTING

Working on circular needles

With right side of work facing you, pick up required number of stitches onto the needle ends. Spread them out along the plastic wire. If the stitches are stretched, either use double-pointed needles or a shorter circular needle. Place a marker onto the first stitch so you know where the round starts and ends. Bring needles together and knit the first stitch pulling the yarn tight to prevent a gap. Keep knitting, sliding the work along the wire as you go until you reach the marker. One round is now complete.

Working with double-pointed needles

Another way of circular knitting is to use double-pointed needles. Use a set of four or even five for larger numbers of stitches. Remember one needle – the working needle – always remains empty so in the case of four needles, divide the number of stitches to be picked up or cast on by 3. The stitch numbers would be divided by 4 if using 5 needles.

1 Using 4 dpns, divide the number of stitches to be picked up by three. If there are 60 stitches in total then you will have 20 stitches on each needle.

2 With the right side of work facing you, pick up 20 stitches on each needle and arrange needles into a triangle shape. Place a marker on the first stitch so you know where the round starts and ends. Then knit across the first 20 stitches using the empty/working needle, making sure to pull the first stitch tight to prevent gaps. Now the needle originally holding the first 20 stitches will be empty. Use this needle to knit across the second 20 stitches. Now the second needle will be empty. Use this needle to knit across the third 20 stitches and to marker. One round is complete.

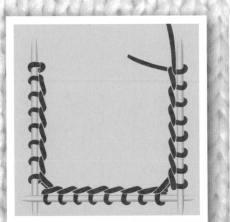

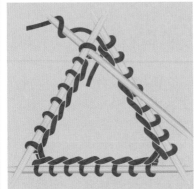

finishing touches

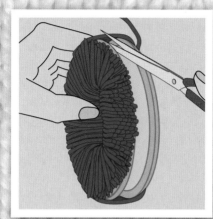
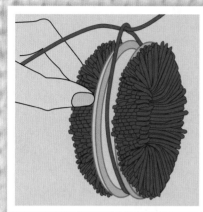

POMPOMS

1 Cut out two cardboard circles a little smaller in diameter than the pompom you want. Make a hole in the middle of both about a third of the diameter. Put both circles together and using lengths of yarn, thread through the middle and begin wrapping around the outer edge until your card is completely covered. Use one or multi-colours for different effects. Continue in this way until the centre hole is only a pinprick.

2 Now for the tricky bit. With sharp-ended scissors, cut all around the edge of the circle, slicing through all the strands.

3 Then ease a longer length of yarn between the card discs and tie very firmly around the centre leaving a tail for sewing. You have now secured all the strands of yarn around the middle. Gently ease the card discs over the pompom and fluff out all the strands before trimming off any loose or straggly ends. Use the long tail to sew onto finished project.

SWISS DARNING (DUPLICATE STITCH)

Swiss darning is great for working small motifs because it looks as if it's been knitted into the fabric.

Horizontal stitches

Work along the row from right to left. Bring threaded needle to front of work at base of the 'V' of the knitted stitch. Pass needle (working from right to left) in and out of the stitch in the row above. Then bring needle back to front of work at base of 'V' and push gently through to back. Repeat for each stitch across the row.

Vertical stitches

Work from bottom to top of row. Bring needle out at base of 'V' as before. Complete the stitch as above but then bring the needle up at base of stitch above and continue working upwards along the line of knitted stitches.

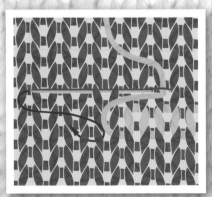

FRENCH KNOT

Work in any direction.

1 Bring needle to RS of fabric. Holding thread taut with finger and thumb of left hand, wind thread once or twice around needle tip.

2 Still holding thread, insert needle tip close to the point where you brought the needle out to the RS of fabric and pull needle to back of work so the twist lies neatly on the fabric surface. Repeat as required.

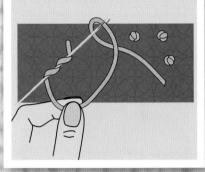

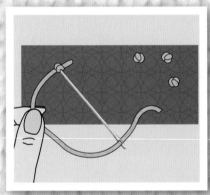

BACK STITCH

Working from right to left.

Bring needle up to right side of work at point **A**, down at point **B** and back up at **C**. Try to keep the distance between stitches even. Begin next stitch at point **C**. Repeat as required.

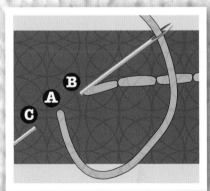

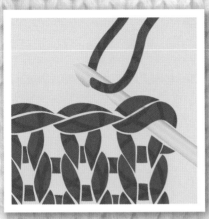

CROCHET EDGING

With a crochet edging, you will be inserting the crochet hook directly into the knitted edge of the fabric you are working on.

1 Begin with the right side of the fabric facing you and start at the right-hand corner edge. Insert your hook through the fabric from front to back and as close to the edge as you can. Make a slip stitch by taking your new yarn and wrapping it round the hook from back to front. Now draw the hook back through the fabric towards you with the loop still on it.

2 Wrap the yarn round the hook for a second time and draw the hook through the first loop on the hook. You will be left with just one loop on the hook and your first stitch.

3 Push your hook through the fabric as before and work an even row of double crochet as follows: wrap new yarn round the hook and draw the loop back through your work towards you. You will now have 2 loops on your hook.

4 Wrap the yarn round the hook once more and draw the hook through both loops. You are now left with only one loop on your hook. This is one double crochet stitch. Continue working in this way until you have worked all around the edge of your garment.

5 Fasten off by breaking the yarn, threading it through your remaining loop and pulling tight.

conversions

GARMENT CARE

After having taking such love and care making your baby's garment, it only follows that you take the same care when washing too. In this way, it should remain looking as fresh and lovely as the day you finished the last stitch.

Always check the ball band of the yarn to see which method of washing is recommended. For instance, a garment made in 100% pure wool might felt and shrink if washed in the machine at high temperature. In this instance, gentle hand washing might be a better method.

SWTC's Amaizing was specially developed with children in mind and can definitely be machine washed at low temperature, which is always a time-saver, but if you are not sure, then I would choose hand washing as your preferred method.

However you wash your garment, take care to dry it flat on an absorbent surface such as a towel to soak up excess moisture. Don't be tempted to put it in a tumble drier or hang it over a radiator. Dry flat and ease into shape.

KNITTING NEEDLE CONVERSIONS

UK	Metric	US
14	2mm	0
13	2.25mm	1
12	2.75mm	2
11	3mm	–
10	3.25mm	3
–	3.5mm	4
9	3.75mm	5
8	4mm	6
7	4.5mm	7
6	5mm	8
5	5.5mm	9
4	6mm	10
3	6.5mm	10.5
2	7mm	10.5
1	7.5mm	11
0	8mm	11
00	9mm	13
000	10mm	15

CROCHET HOOK CONVERSIONS

UK	Metric	US
8	4mm	G/6
9	3.5mm	E/4

YARN WEIGHT CONVERSIONS

UK	US
4-ply	Sport
Double knitting	Light worsted
Aran	Fisherman/Worsted
Chunky	Bulky
Super Chunky	Extra Bulky

abbreviations

alt	alternate		**PM**	place marker
approx	approximately		**P2tog**	purl 2 together
beg	beginning		**psso**	pass slipped stitch over
BO	bind or cast off		**PUK**	pick up and knit
cbbk	cable back		**rem**	remaining
CC	contrast colour		**rep**	repeat
cbfr	cable forward		**RH**	right-hand
cm	centimetres		**rnd**	round
cn	cable needle		**RS**	right side
cont	continue		**sl**	slip
dc	double crochet		**sl st**	slip stitch
dec	decrease		**ssk**	Slip the next 2 sts knitwise. With the left-hand needle, insert into front of these 2 sts and knit them together
DK	double knit			
dpns	double pointed needles			
htr	half treble		**st(s)**	stitch(es)
inc	increase by working into front and back of same stitch		**St st**	stocking stitch
			tog	together
in	inches		**WS**	wrong side
K	knit		**YO**	yarn over
kfb	increase by working into front and back of same stitch		**Yf**	yarn forward
			*	work instructions immediately following *, then rep as directed
K2tog	decrease by knitting 2 stitches together			
Kwise	by knitting the st		[ ]	rep instructions inside brackets as many times as instructed
meas	measures			
MC	main colour			
P	purl			
patt	pattern			

suppliers

ARTESANO LTD
5–9 Berkeley Avenue
Reading
Berkshire
RG1 6EL
UK
tel: +44 (0) 118 9503350
e-mail: info@artesanoyarns.co.uk
www.artesanoyarns.co.uk

CORNISH ORGANIC WOOL
45 Causewayhead
Penzance
Cornwall
TR18 2SS
UK
tel: +44 (0)1736 350905
e-mail: info@cornishorganicwool.co.uk
www.cornishorganicwool.co.uk

INJABULO Fair Trade Buttons
Home Farm Cottage
Ashton Wold, Oundle
Peterborough
PE8 5LZ
UK
tel: +44 (0)1832 274881
e-mail: info@injabulo.com
www.injabulo.com

BLUE SKY ALPACAS INC
PO Box 88
Cedar
MN 55011
USA
tel: 763-753-5815/ 888-460-8862
e-mail: info@blueskyalpacas.com
www.blueskyalpacas.com

HOUSE OF HEMP
Beeston Farm
Marhamchurch
Cornwall
EX23 0ET
UK
tel: +44 (0)1288 381638
e-mail: shopping@houseofhemp.
co.uk
www.houseofhemp.co.uk

MARY GOLDBERG Ceramic Buttons
Stockwell Farm
St Dominick
Saltash
Cornwall
PL12 6TF
UK
tel: +44 (0)1579 351035
e-mail: mary@stockwellpottery.co.uk
www.stockwellceramics.co.uk

**SOUTH WEST TRADING
COMPANY (SWTC)**
918, S Park Lane
Suite 102
Tempe, AZ85281
USA
tel: (866) 794 1818
e-mail: info@soysilk.com
UK stockist: www.angelyarns.co.uk

acknowledgements

FOR GMC PUBLICATIONS

Photography by Chris Gloag,
assisted by Adam Cook.
Flat photography by GMC Publications.
Illustrations by Simon Rodway.
Pattern checking by Carol Chambers.

Thanks to the following babies and
toddlers, and to their mummies and
daddies, for allowing us to photograph
them for this book: Edward, Hannah,
Imogen, Izabella, Jack, Lucien, Seb,
Tabitha and Victoria.

AUTHOR'S ACKNOWLEDGEMENTS

Thanks must go to Gerrie Purcell
at GMC for having the vision to
commission this book in the first
place. Also, thanks to Virginia Brehaut
for excellent editorial skills, Carol
Chambers for her fine maths brain and
pattern checking ability and to Gilda
Pacitti who made such a wonderful job
of the book's styling and art direction.

Special thanks goes to all those who
shared enthusiasm for the project and
donated yarn and notions. I hope I
have done you all proud: Tom Comber
of Artesano, Jonelle and Kat at South
West Trading Company, Jane Blonder
at House of Hemp, Julia and Matt
Hopson at Cornish Organic Wool, Mary
Goldberg at Stockwell Pottery.

A huge, big thanks to Chris Gloag who
took such beautiful photographs. To all
our cute and wonderful models. We
couldn't have done it without you.

To my daughter Emily and her
boyfriend Steven for hours of skein-
winding duties. To my wonderful mum,
Brenda White, and neighbour Michelle
Palmer for deciphering my patterns
and knitting many of the finished
projects. To my ever patient husband
and children, Emily, James and Lucy
for putting up with woolly talk for months
on end. And finally, to Lily; my surprise
bundle who started the whole thing.
May the earth you inherit stay as
beautiful as you are.

index

To request a full catalogue of GMC titles, please contact:

**GMC Publications Ltd, Castle Place, 166 High Street, Lewes, East Sussex, BN7 1XU, United Kingdom
Tel: +44 (0)1273 488005 Fax: +44 (0)1273 402866 www.gmcbooks.com**